LEADERSHIP AND THE SCHOOL LIBRARIAN

ESSAYS FROM LEADERS IN THE FIELD

Mary D. Lankford, Editor

Professional Development Resources for
K-12 Library Media and Technology Specialists

Library of Congress Cataloging-in-Publication Data

Leadership and the school librarian : essays from leaders in the field / [compiled by] Mary D. Lankford.
    p. cm.
 Includes bibliographical references.
 ISBN 1-58683-191-7 (pbk.)
 1. School libraries--United States--Administration. 2. Leadership. I. Lankford, Mary D. II. Title.
Z675.S3L383 2006
025.1'978--dc22
                          2005034166

Published by Linworth Publishing, Inc.
480 East Wilson Bridge Road, Suite L
Worthington, Ohio 43085

Copyright © 2006 by Linworth Publishing, Inc.

All rights reserved. The reproduction of any part of this book for an entire school or school system or for commercial use is strictly prohibited. No part of this book may be electronically reproduced, transmitted, or recorded without written permission from the publisher.

ISBN: 1-58683-191-7

5 4 3 2 1

ABOUT THE AUTHORS

Mary Lankford is an author and library consultant. She is the former director of libraries for the Texas Education Agency. She served as director of library and media services for Irving Independent School district in Texas and as adjunct professor for the School of Library and Information Studies at University of North Texas and Texas Woman's University. She has a Master's of Library Science degree from Texas Woman's University and a Bachelor of Arts degree from the University of North Texas in Denton. She is the recipient of many awards such as the Grolier Foundation Award, American Library Association, 2002; the University of North Texas Distinguished Alumni Award, 1992; and the 1991 AASL/EBE National School Library Media Program of the Year Award. She is the author of several books.

JoAnne Moore began working as an adjunct Texas Library Connection and Library Specialist in 1995. She has served as a contract consultant with the Texas Education Agency and as a library director in Amarillo ISD and Dallas ISD, as well as a school librarian at all grade levels. Her classroom teaching experience includes reading and language arts at the elementary and junior high levels. Ms. Moore supports, maintains and trains TLC members in Region 13 and reports information to Region 13, the Texas Library Connection Information Center and the Texas Education Agency. She also plans other library related workshops in the areas of collection development, weeding, technology applications, copyright, time management, leadership and facility planning for the librarians in Region 13. She has a BBA from West Texas University, a Master's of Education with majors in English and Clinical Reading, Library Certification from Texas Women's University and Supervisor's Certification from Texas Tech University.

Betty Carter is a school librarian in Spring Branch Independent School District, Houston, Texas. She is a professor of children's and young adult literature at Texas Woman's University in Denton, Texas. She lives in Coppell, Texas.

Jim Hundemer has been with the Houston Independent School District for 21 years. He was a social studies high school teacher at Yates High School. He developed a magnet school in communications that now has more than 300 students enrolled. Hundemer moved to central administration as director of communications in 1980 and developed district-wide communication operations as well as HISD's current cable channel. He became assistant superintendent for instructional media services. Hundemer left the district for 10 years to pursue a career in private business and returned in 1998 as manager of the department of library services.

Mary Frances Long has been a middle school teacher-librarian for more than 13 years. Serving as adjunct Professor for Texas Woman's University, Long has taught Librarians as Instructional Partners, School Library Media Center, and Multimedia Materials and School Libraries. She is completing her dissertation, the final stage towards earning a Doctorate in Education with a concentration in Instructional Technology and Distance Education (ITDI) at Nova Southeastern University. Long earned both her Master's in Library Science and Bachelor of Science in Interdisciplinary Studies in Human Ecology from Texas Woman's University. Long believes the destiny of school libraries lies in the hands of the professionally trained and skilled teacher-librarians who recognize the importance of strengthening their role as curriculum and instructional leaders.

Marybeth Green is a middle school librarian in San Antonio, Texas. She has a Bachelor's degree in Education and Master's in Library Science from the University of Texas. She is a doctoral candidate at Texas A&M University. She has served as Chair of the Texas Association of School Librarians, and Regional Director of the American Association of School Librarians. She helped author *Information Power: Building Partnerships for Learning and Information Literacy Standards for Student Learning*. She co-chaired the national AASL conference in 2001. She is a Master Teacher in the NTTI program.

Barbara Bertoldo earned a Library Science Endorsement from the University of Nebraska and a Master's of Library and Information Science from the University of Texas at Austin. She also holds a Bachelor of Arts in English and a Master of Arts in English from Utah State University. She is currently the librarian at Alamo Heights High School in San Antonio. Bertoldo was the Texas Library Connection Information Center and Texas statewide resource-sharing project coordinator in 2000-2001. She has experience with IPTV and online instructional module development and Web page development. She was NewsBank Online Database Consultant from 1996-1999 and served as a curriculum specialist and staff development presenter. She was also the Web-based instructional lessons developer for core curricular areas at Robert E. Lee High School Library, NEISD from 1992-2000.

TABLE of CONTENTS

ABOUT THE AUTHORS 3

INTRODUCTION
    Mary Lankford
        My Background 9
        Finding Leadership Sources 10
        What Makes a Good Leader? 11
            Setting Goals and Taking Responsibility 11
            Advocating 11
            Accepting Change 11
            Managing Time 12
            Networking 13
        Purpose of This Book 13
        Works Cited 14
        Additional Resources 14

CHAPTER 1: LEADERSHIP NATURE OR NURTURE
    Mary Lankford
        Critical Attributes of Leadership 15
            Liberate Staff 15
            Find Ideas 16
            Have Passion 16
            Continue Education and Learning 16
            Be Accountable and Organized 16
        Types of Leaders 17
            Business Leaders 17
            Political Leaders 18
            Domestic Leaders 18
            Historical Leaders 18
        The Final Word on Nature or Nurture 20
        Works Cited 20

CHAPTER 2: CRITICAL ATTRIBUTES OF LIBRARY LEADERS
Mary Lankford

- Integrity and Confidence 23
- A Positive Attitude and Perseverance 23
- A Mission Statement 24
- Working Well with Others 25
- A Need to Learn 25
- Time Management and Organizational Skills 25
- Knowledge of Standards 26
- Conclusion 27
- Works Cited 28

CHAPTER 3: ADVOCACY FOR SCHOOL LIBRARIES
JoAnn Moore

- Definition of Advocacy 29
- School Administrators 31
- Vision and Mission of Texas School Libraries 35
- Advocacy as a Political Activity 36
- Advocacy Tools from Associations and Organizations 39
- Advocacy as a Role within a Campus Setting 40
- Advocacy as a Role within a Community Setting 43
- Formation of Friends Group 44
- Advocacy with Other Types of Educational Institutions 44
- Advocacy for School Libraries by State Libraries 45
- Advocacy Action Plan 46
- Advocacy, a Story with Demonstrated Results 48
- Conclusion 52
- Works Cited 53
- Additional Resources 56

CHAPTER 4: COLLECTION DEVELOPMENT
Betty Carter

- Creating a Collection Development Plan 57
- What Is My Mission? 58
- Who Are My Patrons? 59
- What Kinds of Materials Will Be Included in the Collection? 59
- How Will the Materials Be Selected? 60
- Retrospective Selection 61
- Ongoing Selection 63
- Intellectual Freedom 69
- Deselecting Materials 70
- How Will the Budget Be Allocated? 71
- Works Cited 72
- Additional Resources 73

CHAPTER 5: FINANCIAL SUPPORT AND LIBRARY PROGRAMS
Jim Hundemer

    Building Your Case.. 76
    Putting It Together and Presenting Your Plan.................................. 77
    The Budget... 79
    Now You Have Your Program—What's Next?.................................. 80
    It Will All Collapse without Training...................................... 81
    And, of Course, All Librarians Are Perfect.................................. 82
    Finally, Go Looking for More Money...................................... 83

CHAPTER 6: COLLABORATION
Mary Frances Long

    Collaborative Work Is Never Done.. 85
    Information Power Sets the Stage.. 86
    Influence Through Leadership.. 86
    Leadership Is Learnable.. 87
    The Labor of Collaborating.. 87
    The Choice Is Yours... 88
    Works Cited.. 88

CHAPTER 7: PROFESSIONAL DEVELOPMENT
Mary Beth Green

    Professional Development Best Practices................................... 91
    Coherent Vision.. 91
    Data Driven Content.. 92
    Collaborative Model... 93
    Reflective Practice.. 94
    Active Learning.. 94
    Providing Follow-Up Support.. 95
    Professional Development Format....................................... 95
    Evaluation.. 98
        Participants' Reactions... 98
        Participants' Learning... 98
        Organizational Culture.. 99
        Use of New Skills.. 99
        Student Outcomes... 99
    Tips for Planning an Effective Professional Development Program................ 100
    Look for Opportunities.. 101
    Summary.. 102
    Works Cited... 102

CHAPTER 8: LEARNER-CENTERED TEACHING: INFORMATION ACCESS AND LEADERSHIP
Barbara Bertoldo

- The Librarian as Teacher 106
  - *Case Study A* 107
- The Librarian as Innovator and Collaborator 108
  - *Case Study B* 108
- The Librarian as Part of the Administrative Team 108
  - *Case Study C* 108
- The Librarian as Leader, Listening, Identifying, Creating Opportunities 109
  - *Case Study D* 109
- Information Access & Literacy 110
  - *Case Study E* 111
- Program Administration By the Library Media Specialist 113
- Program Administration Using Technology 116
  - *The Library vs. the Web* 116
  - *Case Study F* 119
- Program Administration Beyond the Library Walls 122
- Works Cited 125

CHAPTER 9: EVALUATION AND REFLECTION
Mary Lankford

- Librarian Certification 130
- Certification and State School Library Standards 130
- Portfolio Development 130
- Reflection 131
- Works Cited 132

TABLE OF FIGURES

7.1	Guskey's Model for the Evaluation Process	99
8.1	Professional Development Checklist	109
8.2	Learner-centered Professional Development Schematic	110
8.3	Generational Learning Characteristics	112
8.4	Facility Space for 21st Century Learners	114
8.5	Ground Rules for Collaboration	115
8.6	Visual Display	117
8.7	Evidence-based Measures	124

INTRODUCTION
Mary Lankford

My Background

Where do you get your ideas? This question is frequently asked of authors, but identifying an idea has never been a problem for me. Ideas are found in many places and I find reading many professional periodicals and books, researching subjects for the children's books I write, and also searching databases and good Web sites have formed mine. There are so many topics I am interested in, and as a librarian who enjoys sharing knowledge, I want everyone to know about the library-related topics that interest me. One of those topics is leadership. Leadership is important in the business world, and it is just as important in the field of education. Little did I know how interested in leadership I have been throughout my career. Although I did not realize it at the time, all the workshops I have conducted over the past 30 years have had the thread of leadership woven through the topics. Those topics include:

- *advocacy*
- *collection development*
- *fiscal management*
- *collaboration*
- *professional development*
- *curriculum integration*
- *time management*
- *technology, and*
- *library management*

I have addressed these topics during a career that has included a wide variety of library positions most likely similarly shared by many of this book's readers. I have worked as a multischool building librarian; a first grade through 8th grade librarian; a district library director; an adjunct college teacher for two different universities; the director of the technology and library division of a state agency; and as an independent school library consultant.

Throughout my career, I found that a basic requirement in the foundation of leadership skills is the ability to ask the question "Why?" Adaptation, change, and questioning the status quo are thinking skills that school librarians must practice every day. My career changes were predicated on the moves made by my husband; however, at each new position, the progress made in developing library programs occurred because I questioned the status quo and identified new methods of building a library program. My foundation in leadership began in the library field prior to the changing roles of women in the workforce. With four children, I used the questioning method and questioned myself (as did my husband) about how to balance home and career. The book *Forget Perfect* (McLeod & Neely, 2005) should have been written in the 1960s for those of us who were trying to keep the balance in our lives and careers without drowning in a sea of guilt. I also questioned myself on the "why" of my actions and found that the answer was that I felt passionately about building a library program similar to the one I enjoyed as an elementary school student. I knew that my children were missing opportunities to experience a library and obtain research skills because they were attending a school without a central library. Because I had this passion, I continued to work in school libraries. I was lucky to have the opportunity to start many library programs because much of the work I did throughout my career was original, in that no one else had been in my position prior to my filling that role.

So, you wonder, why should you care about my background? I outlined my background to show you that my career has provided me with a rich source of material on leadership and has given me knowledge to share with you and, hopefully, help you in developing your leadership skills.

Finding Leadership Sources

During the career I outlined above, while a library director at the district and state level, I had the opportunity to observe librarians. Some of these librarians were individuals I would employ (without hesitation) after talking with them or observing them in their library. What made the difference between a good librarian and an outstanding librarian? I have also had the opportunity to work with educational leaders. Why were some of those administrators just doing their job and others outstanding at their job? I found that all of the outstanding librarians or administrators I observed modeled good leadership skills.

Where do outstanding librarians and administrators learn these leadership skills? One way is to keep reading professional periodicals and books. If you begin collecting information on leadership, you will find, just as I have, that many of the same threads or ideas are repeated in sources aimed at school librarians and also in sources that are not directly aimed at school librarians. Because of this, school librarians hoping to be good leaders should read a wide variety of material. Leadership ideas may come from a biography of Ernest Shackleton, or one of the national business leaders such as Warren Bennis. Additionally, do not exclude other professional organizations in your search for leadership information. The American Society for Training & Development, Inc., the National League for Nursing, Inc., and magazines such as *Presentations* provide articles and editorials on the subject of leadership. Also make sure to check the professional magazines you receive or the databases you have access to for leadership articles. The works cited in this book will include many articles and books with ideas describing how leadership must be implemented. The articles and books may not mention school libraries, but leaders should read everything and translate the ideas to their needs. The ability to read a book, designated for commercial businesses, and translate those ideas to school libraries and education is an essential leadership skill.

Educators need resources to help them learn leadership skills and to provide examples of those skills. Who in your building needs this information? Certainly the librarian, but administrators and teachers can improve their skills through leadership articles as well. The resource file you build should be available to all personnel in the building. This book is based on my readings, my observations, and my identification of how good leadership skills can aid in creating an exemplary school library program while it also will benefit anyone interested in becoming a good leader.

What Makes a Good Leader?

In creating my leadership file and reading sources, I have identified some skills that make a good leader. These skills include the ability to set goals, to be responsible and proactive, to advocate, to accept change, to manage time, and to collaborate.

Setting Goals and Taking Responsibility

Developing a mission statement and setting goals is now a natural part of building a library program and is a skill of a good leader. Brian Tracy titled his book with that one word "Goals." His very clear explanation of what goals will do for you, including increasing confidence, and boosting your level of motivation are the very foundation for leadership (2003, p. 21). My husband has a mantra for young people that states, "You are responsible." If we all assume that we are responsible for our lives, our career, the library program, we will not waste time blaming the administration, or some other group for the problems in developing the library program. Tracy (2003, p. 23) explains that blaming someone else diminishes your power. In Wilson and Lyders, (2001) book on leadership in the school library they state, "Good leadership, then, implies an involvement with people, a sharing (or at least a give and take) of responsibility, a 'bringing along' of others to make good things happen" (p. 3).

Another important reason to improve leadership skills is being proactive and taking action prior to learning that budget or personnel cuts have threatened the library program. It is certainly easier before budget cuts are in place than after to acquire skills that reinforce information about justifying the budget, becoming an advocate, and identifying essential skills in your own professional development. These all may be skills that help you save your job!

Advocating

Now, more than ever in school library history, librarians must assume leadership, not only of the library program in their school, but also leadership in shaping education within the school, and most important, leadership of their own career. In the spring 2004 issue of *Library Media Connection* I wrote an article titled "Weather Vanes, Warning Signs, and Wailing" (Lankford, 2004). In view of the recent hurricanes the article is even timelier today. However, I was only using the weather as a metaphor for the action librarians should take as advocates for exemplary library programs.

I hope school librarians and library educators will see this book as a tool for creating a change in attitude for school librarians. Just as I said in the article, we cannot wait for someone else to board up the windows or secure the property. Now is the time for each librarian to take action, become an advocate, and acquire the leadership skills that will move us forward with the other changes taking place in education.

Accepting Change

I have heard people criticize the "old" librarians for not accepting new technology. Librarians in the 1960s were eagerly accepting of filmstrip projectors, 8mm film loops, and learning how to thread 16mm projectors. This was the "new" technology. Now it is MP3 players, Web blogs, and RSS feeds. Good leaders must have the vision to look forward and accept change, including new technology. The excitement of working with students, teachers, and administrators and with all the outstanding books and databases available should be enough to keep the librarian excited about coming to work each day.

Managing Time

Managing time is another talent of a good leader. In the May issue of *Presentations* the editor in chief, Tad Simmons, titled his editorial "Can a Flesh-Eating Virus Solve Your Weight Problems Forever?" I quote, in part, from his editorial because it points out to librarians that the time we have to present to students, teachers, and administrators is always limited. How do we utilize this time to our advantage? Simmons' title was whimsical and certainly created more interest than something mundane such as "The first two minutes of a presentation are critical." Simmons writes:

> *Not many human endeavors heap more significance on the first two minutes than a presentation. Football players, for instance, have the luxury of floundering around for two or three quarters before their mistakes start to matter. Nail the first two minutes of your speech and your salvation is all but guaranteed; blow them and you'll spend what feels like an eternity trying to recapture the promise and redemption of those initial few moments.*

> *Far too many objectives must be achieved in the first few minutes of a presentation. Rapport with the audience, eye contact, credibility, character and competence all have to be established almost instantaneously, and the speaker's subject matter must be so compelling that it transforms the collective psychology of the room, displacing the perpetual chatter in people's brains with nothing more than the sound of the speaker's voice.*

> *Word choice is everything. The fact of the matter is that most "busy" people, though they may be loathe to admit it, are just trying to keep themselves occupied until something worth paying attention to comes along.*

> *Most work engages the brain about as fully as a game of "Candyland." The presenter's only real challenge, in most cases, is coming up with something to say that's more interesting than a trip to the Peppermint Forest.*

> *That's not so hard, is it?*

> *No, and it shouldn't be. True, the beginning of any presentation is the most important part, but an effective presentation doesn't have to start with a shout or an explosion. The presenter doesn't have to declare a revolution, promise a life-changing cure or pave anyone's way to quick riches. All a presenter needs to do to gain an audience's attention is offer people the gift of a few moments free of the clutter and din of their humdrum daily existence. Give them something meaningful, important or entertaining to listen to, and they will. Why? Because they're hungry for escape. All you have to do is feed them (2005, p. 4).*

Networking

Throughout the years I have had opportunities to network with the librarians who have contributed to this book and with many others. Networking, within your school district and through professional organizations, allows you to see leadership in action. State and national library organizations require involvement of membership. As an involved members leadership skills flourish. Do not just pay your dues and attend the annual conference. Become involved and contribute to professional development for your peers. Through listservs and e-mail, the opportunity is available for networking as never before possible. It is up to you. You are responsible for your professional growth and for the development of leadership skills.

Purpose of This Book

Professional books are expensive. Why should you spend budget money on a book that is not for children? Ask a carpenter how he can do without a hammer? Ask a chef if he doesn't need to continue to read cookbooks. Ask yourself how long it has been since you attended a college course in the field of library and information science? Compare that date to today's date. Has anything changed in technology or library programs since then? Taking time to thoroughly read and understand a professional book allows you to hone skills.

In addition to honing skills, you may need leadership skills to save your job! Today, educators ask questions about why students cannot read or do not make progress on standard achievement or state-mandated tests. In some states the administrative leadership of the school may be replaced if student achievement does not improve. The role of school librarians should not be consumed with improving student test scores; there are many other aspects of the librarians' role that are just as important. However, if librarians plan to remain a crucial part of the answer to improving student achievement, their leadership skills must be evident to administrators, to teachers, to students, and to the community. This book will help librarians find ideas and utilize leadership skills in advocacy, collaboration, instruction, literature guidance, curriculum development, and professional development.

The librarian, in a school setting, can be the most important person on the campus. The principal is the administrative leader; however, there must be collaborative efforts of the librarian to support the principal. As the librarian demonstrates leadership techniques, the administrative leader will become more effective and will assume the advocacy role all school librarians' desire.

As you can see, the multifaceted work of a librarian spans many diverse topics and requires effective leadership skills. This book focuses on the most essential of these topics (advocacy, collection development, collaboration, financial support, instruction, and professional development) and will show how acquiring good leadership skills will benefit you in the development of a good school library program.

Works Cited

Carter, B. (2000). *Best books for young adults* (2nd ed.). Chicago: American Library Association.

Lankford, M. (2004). Weather vanes, warning signs, and wailing. *Library Media Connection,* 22:7, 26-27.

McLeod, L. E., & Neely, J. S. (2001). *Forget perfect: Finding joy, meaning, and satisfaction in the life you've already got and the you you already are.* New York: Perigee Books.

Simmons, T. (2005). Can a flesh-eating virus solve your weight problems forever? *Presentations,* May, 4.

Tracy, Brian. (2003). *Goals! How to get everything you want faster than you ever thought possible.* San Francisco: Berrett Koehler Publishers, Inc.

Wilson, P. P., & Lyders, J. A. (2001). *Leadership for today's school library: A handbook for the library media specialist and the school principal.* Westport: Greenwood Press.

Additional Resources

Bennis, W. (1989). *On becoming a leader* (Updated and Expanded ed.). New York: Basic Books.

Gardner, H. (2004). *Changing minds: The art and science of changing our own and other people's minds.* Boston: Harvard Business School Press.

Maine Association of School Librarians. (1998). *SLMS evaluation action plan.* Retrieved September 7, 2005, from http://www.maslibraries.org/resources/slmseval/slmseval.html.

CHAPTER ONE: LEADERSHIP NATURE or NURTURE

Mary Lankford

Are leaders born or do they learn the skill of leadership? I believe leadership skills can be learned. I do understand that many people have a well-developed sense of self-confidence at an early age; however, I believe that self-confidence can be gained through exercising the critical attributes of leadership.

Critical Attributes of Leadership

What are the critical attributes of leadership? A critical attribute is something that remains constant. A critical attribute of life is death. This fact does not change. We can contribute to an early death by reckless behavior and poor health habits, but no matter what measures we take death is certain. The critical attributes of leadership include the ability: to liberate staff, to find ideas, to have passion, to continue education and learning, and to be accountable and organized.

Liberate Staff

The puzzle of leadership is defined as an art in the book *Leadership Is an Art* by Max DePree. "The art of leadership," as DePree (1989) says, is "liberating people to do what is required of them in the most effective and humane way possible. Thus, the leader is the 'servant' of his followers in that he removes the obstacles that prevent them from doing their jobs. In short, the true leader enables his or her followers to realize their full potential" (p. xviii).

How do we liberate people to do what is required of them in the most effective and humane way possible? One way to liberate people is to have clear and concise descriptions of their jobs duties. In the school library we may be fortunate enough to have adult clerical staff, volunteers, or student assistants. If you write out the tasks required of the people working with you in the library, can you be specific about the tasks? Do you have a job description for each of the roles? If not, writing the tasks and the job description will provide both you and the library staff with a clear understanding of what expectations you have. A question you should ask about the tasks: Why is this task essential to the operation of the library program? [Think of the task of reshelving books. If all the books are checked out and not ever returned to the shelves it will be difficult to locate the books.] This statement may seem very evident to the library staff, but to a person working for the first time in the library this may seem to be a very dull and unimportant task. Write the steps you use in reshelving books. Does this plan seem reasonable to the new person? If not, why not? Another person looking at a task may find a better way to accomplish the task. Allowing the person to establish a routine—and writing this routine out for the next person—is liberating them to use their sense of order.

Find Ideas

DePree (1989) also cites that "the leader must know his own mind and that is why leadership requires ideas" (p. xix). Thinking about what you do as a library leader and why you do it is an ongoing element of leadership. The statement "We have always done it that way" is not a statement made by a library leader. We are fortunate to live in a time of great diversity, not only of ideas but also of people. We understand that there should be opportunities for everyone to contribute to an exemplary library program. Frequently we have ignored the ideas of the students in the school. The school librarian is a constant in the students' time in school. Students change teachers each year; however, the librarian remains a constant except for the changes between elementary, middle, and high school. Some of the most important work a librarian can do is learn about the students in the school and listen to their ideas.

I agree with DePree (1989) in that "the first responsibility of a leader is to define reality. The last is to say thank you. In between the two, the leader must become a servant and a debtor. That sums up the progress of an artful leader" (p. 9).

Have Passion

In addition to being an artful leader, a school leader must have a passion for what school libraries provide for students and the school staff. Passion is not a word I use lightly. I should, at my age, be sitting on a porch somewhere tending to my knitting, but my passion is school libraries and the improvement of all libraries; therefore, I am still attending workshops, still working with librarians, and still reading professional journals. I hope that my passion, my sincere approach to leadership, will provide a legacy for school librarians of the future. What I describe is not an easy path. The easy path is one that concentrates only on the tasks of checking books in and out, allowing just anyone to select books, and learning the names of only a few students. If you want to be a leader you will look for the more difficult road. However, this road will offer more challenges and you will never state that you are bored.

Continue Education and Learning

Who can you identify as a school library leader? Look at the librarians in your district, your area, your state, and your professional associations. What critical attributes can you identify in these leaders? What relationships do these school library leaders have with other librarians? What is their relationship with the institution that employs them? You can probably recognize a continued interest in learning. If a leader is interested in change and new ideas, they must have a continued interest in education and learning.

Be Accountable and Organized

There are obviously several other attributes effective leaders can possess. Do you see a sense of maturity in the leaders you know? Maturity can also be evidenced in a sense of responsibility. This leader will do what is expected, and you can count on the person. The accountability and organizational ability to do things in a timely manner are additional critical attributes of a leader.

Types of Leaders

Once you know the critical attributes of a leader, we wonder if all types of leaders are the same. Are business leaders, political leaders, and domestic leaders the same as school library leaders? What can we learn from historical leaders and leaders in different fields?

Business Leaders

As we discussed in the Introduction to this book, leadership is as important in business as it is in education. Are the critical attributes of leadership the same in business as in education? To answer that question, I looked to my daughter for information. My oldest daughter received her Master's in Library and Information Science and has always been employed by private corporations. It has been very interesting to me to compare the problems those of us who work with educational institutions believe would be solved if only we worked in a profit-making corporation. As I listen to my daughter's problems as a librarian in a corporate world, I see that not all problems are resolved with profits. Leadership in business is usually predicated on goals and objectives. How time is allocated to a project, how time is managed, and how thoroughly you understand the problem is essential to the corporate perspective. If a job must be done by tonight we will all work until midnight. There is no overtime in the corporate world. The pay scale is much better, but the time spent on the job is longer. I consider my daughter a leader, not because we are related, but because her company rated her a leader. I have given some thought to the critical attributes of her leadership qualities and list them here:

Critical Attributes for a Corporate Library Leader

- *Constantly reading from professional journals, from newspapers, and from magazines.*
- *Striving to improve professionally through staff development provided by the corporation and through professional meetings.*
- *Indepth understanding of the field of employment.*
- *Interest in change and in learning about operations of the company throughout the world.*
- *Accepting and utilizing technology to the maximum.*

The critical attributes described above are also true for school library leaders. Therefore, both corporate and school librarians can benefit from similar resources on leadership. John C. Maxwell, the founder of Injoy, writes one such resource. Injoy is an organization dedicated to helping people maximize their personal and leadership potential. Maxwell is a nationally known speaker and is the author of both books and tapes. In his book, *The 21 Irrefutable Laws of Leadership: Follow Them and People Will Follow You* (Maxwell, 1998) he identifies "The Law of Process" (1998, p. 24) and outlines that leadership growth has four phases. First, people do not recognize the value of leadership. In the second stage when careers place us in leadership situations, we begin to understand what we do not know. The third stage occurs when we determine that we need to improve leadership skills, and we begin to grow and hone those skills. In the fourth and final phase we find that our understanding of leadership skills is automatic and we also understand that we must improve on a continuing basis.

Political Leaders

Political leaders are easily identified and their politics usually reflect their ability to lead. Politics does not only include those elected to office. Politics plays a large role in any school district. The school librarian who does not recognize the political hierarchy is doomed to regret not learning more about working with political groups. The political group may be the parents who lead the school parent teacher organization, or the teachers who determine the fate of the budget of the local site base management team.

Domestic Leaders

Each trip to the grocery story checkout counter will provide magazines with headlines about managing your career, weight loss, time management, and information on the current holiday or new home styles. Domestic leaders wear many hats. The fine line a person walks when managing a career and also giving enough attention to family is perhaps the most difficult skill to learn. School leaders will also have to walk fine lines when managing relationships between the school board, administrators, faculty, students, parents, and others. Domestic leaders and school leaders share this personality management attribute.

Historical Leaders

Biographies of leaders in all fields can give us a perspective of how everyday people achieved the critical attributes of leadership and will be remembered as much for their leadership as for other accomplishments.

In the book *Shackleton's Way* (Morrell & Capparell, 2000) the author uses the subtitle *Leadership Lessons from the Great Antarctic Explorer*. In the book Shackleton is described as reaching nearly every goal he ever set; being praised by all the men who served under him; and successfully leading all the members of his crew to safety after a harrowing two-year fight for their lives. If you ever have the opportunity to suggest a book for the entire staff to read and discuss, this title is most appropriate for improving leadership skills and school climate. Shackleton's list of ways to find determination to move forward provides many ideas for school leaders.

Shackleton's Way of Finding the Determination to Move Forward (Morrell & Capparell, 2000)

- *Go-for-broke risks become more acceptable as options narrow. Sometimes the potential rewards at the end of a daring venture justify suffering a spectacular failure.*

- *Seek inspiration in enduring wisdom that has comforted or motivated you or others in times of crisis. It will get you through the most physically and emotionally draining times and help you to keep your perspective.*

- *Congratulate yourself and others for a job well done. A pat on the back or a sincere handshake is an expression of personal thanks and gratitude that has never gone out of fashion.*

- *Motivate your staff to be independent. If you have been a good leader, they will have the determination to succeed on their own.*

- *Let your staff inspire you. At times, an overwhelming workload may force you to consider lowering your standards. Remember that the final product must represent the best efforts of the entire group.*

> *☞ Even in the most stressful situations, don't forget that you are part of a larger world that might benefit from your expertise. In turn, participating in community and family activities can give you skills useful on the job.*
>
> *☞ Make sure the whole job is done. Your staff may be able to call it quits after the heavy lifting is over, but you are responsible for seeing the work through to its successful completion.*

As we equate Shackleton's ideas for moving forward to building an exemplary library program, the key words in his first idea are "options narrow." If the narrow option facing you is no money for the purchase of resources, the librarian must assume a go-for-broke attitude in obtaining funding for resources. Shackleton's second idea is about inspiration. The librarian gains inspiration through the interaction of teachers, administrators, and other librarians. Reading success stories in professional journals can be inspirational. Attending a professional conference can be inspirational. Perhaps knowing a student who is overcoming obstacles to gain an education can be inspirational. Inspiration can come from many places.

Congratulations are essential to the role of leadership. Examples of this third idea include: a brief written note, a card with a small silk orchid placed in a teacher's mail box, or a candy kiss attached to a business card letting someone know that you could kiss them for their support are just a few of the ways congratulations can be conveyed. The congratulatory phrase given to others will be repaid many times. Do not forget yourself. If your goals are written—do not just cross them off when completed—give yourself a congratulatory prize.

Shackleton's fourth idea urges that we build independence. If we want first grade students to find their way to the library, this independence must be built through taking them through the paces to the library location. A clerk working in the library must be taught the independence of making decisions while the librarian is out of the building. This can be done by working with the clerk to establish a job description and procedures that support independence.

Library standards are in place for a purpose. If Shackleton had lowered his standards, lives might have been lost. What standards in the library must remain in place? How do you establish priorities? Is assisting a student more important than having all books shelved before the library closes?

Giving of your expertise is essential. Throughout your career you will be learning from others. This learning must be passed on to others in the school and in the profession. If an e-mail arrives on a listserv and you have a suggestion to solve the problem, then take time to answer. The stress of the job must never take away from giving back to the profession.

Lastly, Shackleton stresses to make sure the job is done. When is the job completed? If goals have been set you can easily see when the task is done. The librarian must assume the responsibility to see that all work is completed successfully.

The Final Word on Nature or Nurture

So, can leadership skills be learned? The examples provided in this chapter show that leadership can be learned. Some people are born leaders while others have to struggle to become good leaders. In either case, the end result can be the same. Studying the critical attributes of library leaders and reviewing examples of effective leadership skills from business leaders, political leaders, domestic leaders, and historical leaders provides us with several ideas to use in our own growth as a leader. Effective leadership skills cross disciplines and we can learn much from looking outside school libraries and organizations.

Works Cited

DePree, M. (1989). *Leadership is an art*. New York: Doubleday.

Maxwell, J. C. (1998). *The 21 irrefutable laws of leadership: Follow them and people will follow you*. Nashville: Thomas Nelson Publishers.

Morrell, M., & Capparell, S. (2000). *Shackleton's way: Leadership lessons from the great Antarctic explorer*. New York: Penguin Books.

CHAPTER TWO:
CRITICAL ATTRIBUTES
of LIBRARY LEADERS
Mary Lankford

In chapter one we mentioned critical attributes of library leaders. In this chapter we will expand on this idea. Do leaders possess critical attributes? What are critical attributes? "Critical" is defined as "having a decisive or crucial importance or failure of something." "Attribute" is defined as "a quality or feature that is regarded as a characteristic or an inherent part of someone or something" (*New Oxford*, 2005). The phrase "critical attribute" is used here then to describe the essential characteristics of a library leader.

Do men or women have the essential characteristics of a library leader? Is the role of a leader easier for a male or a female? Evans, Layzell Ward, and Rugaas (2000) found, "In 1990, a meta-analysis of all the literature on the subject concluded there were only very small differences (not statistically significant) between men's and women's leadership styles in an organizational setting. What differences that did exist were minor and only in two areas: men were slightly more aggressive and slightly less democratic than women. It would appear there is little or no support for the idea women are generally less able to be effective leaders of organizations" (p. 374).

Clearly this research supports the premise that both men and women can be good leaders, but are all managers good leaders? Specifically, if someone is in a *position* to exert influence does this identify him or her as a leader? In some situations the person occupying the *position* is there through tenure, longevity, or inaccurate evaluation of the person's skills. Frequently people are thrust into a position and must learn leadership skills related to the position. The key word in this statement is *learn*. A school librarian, whether new or a veteran, must commit to learn and hone leadership skills throughout his or her career. Evans et al. (2000) states, "It is unlikely that future researchers will produce a definitive list of a leader's personality traits" (p. 360). The studies of leadership are cited in F. E. Fiedler and the staff at the University of Illinois Group Effectiveness Research Laboratory (qtd. in Evans 2000) as follows: "Three major factors that affect an individual's leadership effectiveness include:

> *1) the leader's power or authority, as defined by the official position held;*
>
> *2) the nature of the work being performed by the group; and*
>
> *3) the personal relationship between the leader and the group"* (p. 375).

Their basic conclusion was not too surprising: "The leader who is liked by his group and has a clear-cut task and high position power…has everything in his favor. The leader who has poor relationships with his group members, an unstructured task and weak position power likely will be unable to exert much influence over the group" (p. 375).

So, based on this information, it is unlikely we will form a definitive list of essential characteristics for a library leader. This can be seen in the observance that leaders come in all shapes and sizes. Each leader will be unique. Leadership styles are personal and must be developed individually. You may work for one manager who is effective for an entirely different reason than a previous manager was. But this does not mean that a list of essential characteristics for leaders is impossible.

In their book *Leadership: A Communication Perspective*, Michael Hackman and Craig Johnson (2000) identified characteristics of transformational leaders as:

- *creative (innovative, foresighted);*
- *interactive (skilled communicators who use power images, metaphors, and models);*
- *vision headed;*
- *empowering (encourage participation and involvement); and*
- *passionate (care deeply for their work).*

The term transformational leadership refers to those leaders who actually transformed the lives of their followers or their society. Think of the lives that were transformed by the leadership of Martin Luther King, Jr. or the life of Mahatma Gandhi.

Bohdan Oppenheim (qtd. in Evans 2000) stated that effective leadership requires "vision, plus values, plus focus, plus persuasion. Leaders write the music, managers conduct the orchestra, producing the beauty from a team effort" (p. 256). Reading books on the subject of leadership is a little like reading books on time management. The content of the book may offer a different view, perhaps something you had not considered because there is little agreement on the definition of leadership.

Even though there is little agreement on the definition of leadership, generally, most leaders have common characteristics that they use in developing their own personal style. Leaders have integrity, confidence, a positive outlook, and the ability to persevere. Along with these personality strengths, they also have a vision of what needs accomplished, the ability to give credit to and work well with others, time management and organizational skills, a continued need to learn, and last, but not least, knowledge of their field.

Integrity and Confidence

A leader must have enthusiasm about their library program and must be able to convey that enthusiasm to others. In *The Leadership Pill* by Blanchard and Muchnick (2003), the authors outline the secret blend for effective leadership, and add that, "Leadership Is Not Something You Do to People; It's Something You Do with Them" (p. 110). The authors of this small and informative book create a bulleted list on effective leadership under the categories of the following:

- *integrity,*
- *partnership,*
- *affirmation, and*
- *perfecting the blend.*

I would certainly add integrity to the list of critical attributes needed to be a school library leader. For example, a football coach told me that to really have integrity you must have only one set of rules. You do not allow a star player to work under one set of rules and use another set of rules for the remaining players. A librarian has many opportunities to use several sets of rules. When you allow a fourth grade teacher to check out all of the books on a key subject because she is friendlier to you than the other teachers in that grade, you have created a special set of rules for her. Your integrity will be challenged as soon as other teachers understand what has happened.

In addition to integrity, confidence is essential. Confidence is something that builds with experience. Confidence is a trait that grows as a person becomes more knowledgeable about their profession. Confidence becomes stronger as decision-making becomes natural and is based on both knowledge and experience. As a professional librarian confidence can be developed through staff development. Many organizations have programs on both decision-making and confidence building.

A Positive Attitude and Perseverance

Banish the term "burn out" from your vocabulary. Why? Because each time you repeat the phrase about yourself you are reinforcing the idea. Use positive remarks to describe your job and what is happening in your school. Education has changed, and will continue to change, just as the role of a librarian has changed. You would not want a quiet library with no one coming in the door. The library has never been a place to *escape*. The library must continue to change to meet the needs of students, teachers, administrators, and the community. The librarian is that catalyst for change. The greater than sign (>) should be engraved on the library sign at the door. We are building students who will be greater than those who were here last year. The library will have resources that are greater than those we had last year.

Of all the character traits we must see in a librarian, one of the most important is perseverance. As Winston Churchill said when Great Britain was suffering daily bombings in World War II "We will never give up." Perseverance is made up of the "P" words:

- *purpose,*
- *personality,*
- *pursuit, and*
- *performance.*

These "P" words are the mortar for the foundation of an exemplary library program. You establish your purpose through a concise mission statement. It is said that personalities shape the age. The personality of the librarian should be open, smiling, flexible, and reliable. Your pursuits are those that enhance the library program. If you know the math teachers are not using the library then you should meet with them and pursue their involvement in the library. This means you go to the math department, request a meeting with the department, and work with individual teachers. Lastly, performance is what is expected of students and teachers. The test-driven society expects student achievement. Student achievement depends not only on the student, but also on the teaching. The library and the librarian must be a part of their performance. Explaining why collaboration is essential is a part of the librarian's performance. If a teacher turns down your initial offer of collaborating, don't give up. Keep in contact with that teacher and continue to find ways that might open a door for a collaborative effort.

A Mission Statement

Along with the personality traits described above, leaders also have a clear sense of what is to be accomplished in their library program. They have this vision by believing in and practicing the development of a mission statement as a precursor for goals. The vision of what is to be accomplished may be a short- or long-term project. The development of an exemplary library program does not happen overnight.

One suggestion for developing a mission statement is to begin with the phrase "My mission is to" and record three action verbs that best describe your project (e.g., accomplish, build, finance, give, discuss). The next step is to identify a principle, a value, or a purpose that you can commit the rest of your life to pursuing (joy, service, faith, creativity, justice). Finish by identifying the group or cause that most excites you (real estate, design, sports, women's issues). "Your final statement ought to inspire you and should direct all your activities, both on and off the job" (Johnson, 2001, p. 63). If we develop a mission statement for our career as a library leader it might look something like this: My mission is to develop an exemplary library program for the XXXX school district by using my expertise, creativity, and passion and by demonstrating to teachers and students that effective use of information can change their lives.

Working Well with Others

A mission statement can only be realized if you are able to work well with and give credit to your team. In the book *Good to Great,* Collins (2001) compiled research on what makes a good company move from being just good to being a great company. In all of the "great" company leaders the research showed that the CEO of the company never wanted any credit for the success of the company. Never wanting credit for success is also true for school librarians. The project was a success, the students achieved their learning objectives, the teachers were pleased, and the librarian was a part of the team.

A Need to Learn

We live in an age where professional reading does not mean a trip to a university or public library. Through online resources we can easily read or download articles from other professions. Librarians are easily on the level with the administrators of the school. If a principal or counselor is reading about confidence, decision making, and leadership then make sure to read their journals to get ideas. The person who states that they do not have time to read the newspaper; read reviews for new books; read books—adult pleasure reading or children's books; read professional periodicals; or read student writing will best be described in a quotation from Diane Ravitch, "The person who knows 'how' will always have a job. The person who knows 'why' will always be his boss." Librarians are not expected to be an expert in every subject, but the exemplary librarian is going to try and be knowledgeable about as many facets of the world as possible. Reading is our edge. Reading is our key to improving ourselves. Reading is the foundation essential to an exemplary library program.

Time Management and Organizational Skills

What if you are having trouble finding time to work with your team or read? Are clutter and low-level tasks taking all your time? A wonderful resource for learning to manage your time is J'aimé L. Foust's book *Dewey Need to Get Organized?* Her many ideas for goal setting, utilizing graphic organizers, and file folders are readable, usable, and apply to all of us who work in a demanding job. I believe goal setting, daily planning, and establishing priorities for the day are the keys to avoiding stress and managing a good library program.

Librarians know that they must handle a variety of interruptions. Once we understand that interruptions are a part of our job, we must then discover ways to eliminate some of the interruptions. As an example, have teachers been given the "password" necessary to override the computer? Why not? If teachers are checking out books for their classroom or assisting students, why can they not be trusted to handle this minor glitch in circulation? The more power you give away (passwords are power) the more power you will have.

Hundreds of pieces of paper pass across the librarian's desk. Must you actually look at all these papers? Teach a member of your team—a library clerk or a student—to sort the mail. Anything from the administration or in the form of a memo will go in one folder for you to examine when you have established time to look at the mail. Any catalogs can be filed according to your established list of catalogs you retain. As the student files the new catalog, the old one is pulled and discarded. If the mail includes "opportunities" from contest companies, they should go straight into the wastebasket.

Time management is a little like playing the piano. You can buy the music, purchase the piano, take lessons, but if you never practice you will never be able to entertain yourself or your friends by playing the piano. Try these techniques. If you are failing, do not give up. Try again the next day until it becomes a habit.

Knowledge of Standards

Leaders also should have a thorough knowledge of their field. In the education world, that includes knowledge of standards. School librarians are indeed fortunate that they have recognized national standards. Most states have standards that reflect state and local needs. Standards, or levels of quality, are not painstakingly written to be purchased and placed on a shelf in the library. Standards are to be studied and used to establish goals and objectives for the library program. *Information Power: Building Partnerships for Learning* provides information literacy standards for student learning, a vision statement, and nine information literacy standards "designed to guide and support library media specialists' efforts in the three major areas: learning and teaching; information access; and program administration" (AASL & AECT, 1998, p. 8). It is important to be thoroughly familiar with these standards even if you are not a member of the national library association. Most states have made their standards available on the Web and it is interesting to search these sites to see how you can utilize the ideas in setting your goals.

There are a number of good resources to help you in learning about standards. Toni Buzzeo (2002), in her book *Collaborating to Meet Standards: Teacher/Librarian Partnerships*, refers to the *Information Power* mandate of collaboration. The term collaboration is also included in all federal grant guidelines. Buzzeo's useful suggestions about overcoming roadblocks to collaboration provide a path down this sometimes rocky road.

Donna Miller (2004) tells us in *The Standards-Based Integrated Library, 2nd Edition* that most state and local standards are derived from national standards. Chapters in her book begin with a citation of the content standards addressed such as the National Council of Teachers of English or National Council of Teachers of Math.

We see standards cited once more in Walter L. McKenzie's (2004) book, *Standards-Based Lessons for Tech-Savvy Students: A Multiple Intelligences Approach*. McKenzie outlines the steps in the development of units of study. The first step is to identify the standard, then the theme, and lastly, a statement of the big idea. From that foundation McKenzie identifies "Need to Know Questions," "The Mission," and ends with "Learning Tasks." The examples in his book provide: standards from more than one subject area, the theme citing the big idea, the need to know questions, and the mission. Learning tasks are diverse and may include: learning through language; learning through problem solving; learning through seeing and imagining; and learning through patterns. The extensive list of examples in McKenzie's book should provide teachers and librarians many ways to use the national standards to support state and local curriculum requirements.

Conclusion

In his book *Lincoln on Leadership*, Phillips (1993) outlines ideas about leadership that can serve school librarians today:

- *Get out of the office and circulate among the troops.*
- *Build strong alliances.*
- *Persuade rather than coerce.*
- *Honesty and integrity are the best policies.*
- *Never act out of vengeance or spite.*
- *Have the courage to handle unjust criticism.*
- *Be a master of paradox.*
- *Exercise a strong hand—be decisive.*
- *Lead by being led.*
- *Set goals and be results-oriented.*
- *Encourage innovation.*
- *Master the art of public speaking.*
- *Influence people through conversation and storytelling.*
- *Preach a vision and continually reaffirm it.*

This is quite an aggressive list of goals for a leader, but all worth aiming to accomplish. We outlined in this chapter some critical attributes of library leaders that fit with the list above. Even though there is little agreement on the definition of leadership, good leaders do have many characteristics in common. Leaders should continually strive to have integrity, confidence, a positive outlook, and the ability to persevere. Leaders should also possess a vision of what needs accomplished, the ability to give credit to and work well with others, time management and organizational skills, a continued need to learn, and a thorough knowledge of their field. If this list is overwhelming, pick just a few and make accomplishing them a goal. When you feel you have made progress on those goals, pick a few more attributes from the list and work on those. Being a good leader is hard work and requires much vigilance of your actions, but the rewards you and your team will receive from this vigilance are worth the effort.

Works Cited

American Association of School Librarians, & Association for Educational Communications and Technology. (1998). *Information power: Building partnerships for learning.* Chicago: American Library Association.

Blanchard, K., & Muchnick, M. (2003). *The leadership pill: The missing ingredient in motivating people today.* New York: Free Press (Simon & Schuster).

Buzzeo, T. (2002). *Collaborating to meet standards: Teacher/librarian partnerships for K-6.* Worthington, OH: Linworth Publishing.

Buzzeo, T. (2002). *Collaborating to meet standards: Teacher/librarian partnerships for 7-12.* Worthington, OH: Linworth Publishing.

Collins, J. (2001). *Good to great.* East Sussex, UK: Gardners Books.

Evans, G. E., Layzell Ward, P., & Rugaas, B. (2000). *Management basics for information professionals.* New York: Neal-Schuman Publishers.

Foust, J. (2002). *Dewey need to get organized? A time management and organization guide.* Worthington, OH: Linworth Publishing.

Hackman, M. Z., & Johnson, C. E. (2000). *Leadership: A communication perspective (3rd ed.).* Prospect Heights, IL: Waveland.

Johnson, C. E. (2001). *Meeting the ethical challenges of leadership: Casting light or shadow* (p. 63). Thousand Oaks, CA: Sage Publications.

McKenzie, W. L. (2004). *Standards-based lessons for tech-savvy students: A multiple intelligences approach.* Worthington, OH: Linworth Publishing.

Miller, D. (2004). *The standards-based integrated library: A collaborative approach for aligning the library program with the classroom curriculum (2nd ed.).* Worthington, OH: Linworth Publishing.

The New Oxford American Dictionary (2nd ed.). (2005). New York: Oxford University Press.

Phillips, D. T. (1993). Lincoln on leadership: *Alternative executive strategies for tough times.* New York: Warner Books.

CHAPTER THREE: ADVOCACY for SCHOOL LIBRARIES

JoAnn Moore

Definition of Advocacy

Advocacy is not a four-letter word. In fact, advocacy has the potential of forever eliminating four letter words. It can bring about the changes we are seeking, and those changes can make a difference in the overall library program and in student achievement. Much of the time, the word advocate looks and acts like a noun, as though it names something or someone. When the advocate takes action, the word becomes a verb. Yes, we can be called advocates, but it is only when we shift to the verb form of advocate and motivate others to do the same that we see results. Advocacy is organized influence. When we advocate, we seek to influence the attitudes of others in planned and organized ways. Ultimately, we hope to motivate others to action.

The American Heritage Dictionary defines advocacy as the "art of pleading" or persuasion. Advocacy is the act of speaking or writing in favor of something. You are developing support for your library program and making a public recommendation. Advocacy includes marketing and public relations. The distinguishing feature of public relations is to push out the services. Marketing is determining what the administrators, the teachers, the parents, and the students want. You want to help your decision makers be successful with *student achievement* and *literacy*. The three steps to advocacy include a good program, identifying and working with the decision makers, and involving others to gain support (Bishop, 2005).

Ken Haycock (1990) defines advocacy "as an ONGOING plan to develop support and understanding through specific and SUSTAINED efforts over TIME incrementally" (n.p.). His definition would be a good one to commit to memory, and in so doing we realize that advocacy must be ongoing and sustained. First, raise awareness. Next, build support and understanding. Then, keep the ball rolling.

Ken Haycock (1990) describes a successful advocator as someone who:

- *loves what they do and loves people;*
- *knows the mission, goals, and issues of their school;*
- *will choose three issues for focus;*
- *will develop an action plan;*
- *will articulate the action plan in the right place at the right time;*
- *is enthusiastic, positive, and persistent;*
- *doesn't whine or complain;*
- *follows through with their commitment;*
- *knows the importance of a written thank you to those who are responsible for successful outcomes; and*
- *demonstrates and communicates the results of having their requests funded. (Haycock 1990)*

Advocacy is a front burner issue in library education, and the Faculty of Information Studies at the University of Toronto broke new ground in education for librarianship by offering a course in Library Advocacy and Issues in the fall term of 2004. Wendy Newman and Valentina Bauer (2005) ask a central question in their article, "Incitement to Advocate: ..." "Shouldn't tomorrow's librarians be equipped to lead effective advocacy for libraries—knowledgeably, skillfully, and passionately?" (p. 41). Knowledge of marketing and advocacy is a trend in both Canada and the United States Advocacy is the planned, sustained marketing of an issue. Because of the number of issues confronting libraries today, it is critical that librarians know how to read and influence decisions that affect libraries. The course syllabus states, "Students will gain the knowledge needed to understand the advocacy process and exercise professional leadership in the advocacy of library issues. Such advocacy may relate to policy, funds, support, or partnership, and may be directed to internal or external decision-makers." The course includes the nature of advocacy, the relationship of advocacy to promotion and marketing, decision-makers' environments and their perceptions of libraries, and the identification and engagement of stakeholders. Major emphasis is on the development of advocacy programs including objectives, target groups, obstacles, communication tools, and evaluation." (Newman & Bauer, p. 41).

According to the American Library Association's *Library Advocacy Now* promotion, advocacy is about saying to decision-makers: "We care about your mission and goals, and we can assist you by what we have to offer." Advocacy is "the process of turning passive support into educated action by stakeholders." A well-developed advocacy program markets, promotes, and rallies people around the mission, issues, and philosophies of your school library media program. As a result, advocacy must be based on specific needs and supported with evidence. One form of advocacy is to advertise what the librarian offers in the school's oasis of reading, researching, and learning, and the other is to promote support for libraries (ALA, 2005).

School Administrators

Research paints a picture of the school administrator as an instructional leader, collaborative facilitator, and visionary. School library advocates ask, "How can we capitalize on our administrator's goals to further our own program goals?" What does the current research say that person should be doing?

Administrators need our help to bridge the gap between their vision and its actualization. Good administrators can convincingly communicate the school's mission to teachers, parents, and students. Your administrator may not understand the goals of the library and how they fit into the school's mission. Thus, it is up to you, the librarian, to communicate the library goals. If you do not have a mission statement for the school library that aligns with the school's mission, develop this fundamental statement of the library's purpose.

Know the principal's goals. Listen when the principal speaks. Frame proposals from the principal's perspective. Do an executive summary and place the bottom line at the top. Be brief (Hartzell, 2003, October). Even though a school district may not require a library report, it is wise to create one by zeroing in on what is most important in student learning. For example, when showing the number of collaborative sessions, describe the lesson objectives, how students demonstrated what they learned, and how the library program contributed to their success. The report becomes a marketing tool for the librarian's role in student achievement (Hartzell, 2003, May).

In reference to how few administrators are library advocates, principal John Titus, in an article titled "Getting in the Principal's Face," stated: "It's about the library media specialist getting in the principal's face. Some librarians don't advocate well" (St. Lifer, 2004, p. 11).

On the flip side, one librarian, echoing the voices of countless other librarians asked, "Is Anybody Out There?" in her letter to the editor of *School Library Journal* in January 2005. She felt she had tried on many occasions to advocate for the library, but she didn't feel she was heard. Her letter reflects the discouragement of many librarians who feel they have talked with principals, but have not received their support (Perkins, 2005, p. 13). A listening ear requires the library advocate to report on facts and figures and information from the studies that show that the role of libraries and expenditures on school librarians does increase student achievement. Librarians do have the responsibility of knowing the mission of the principal and working with the principal and the teachers to accomplish that mission. The librarian has a role to play in student achievement, integrated curriculum, literacy, and the use of technology. Aren't all our goals related?

Significant studies by Lance in Colorado, Lance and Loertscher in Pennsylvania and Oregon, and Smith in Texas during 2001 showed positive correlations between student achievement and library services administered by a professionally certified librarian. Characteristics of the library program and the librarian provide an understanding of what is necessary (Hartzell, 2003, December).

Site-based management focuses reform and restructuring efforts on those closest to the students. On the positive side, the librarian shares decision-making with administrators and other teachers as:

- *a partner in instruction;*
- *budgeting;*
- *program planning;*
- *collection development;*
- *collaboration with classroom teachers;*
- *understanding technology as a tool in teaching and learning;*
- *providing information and relevant resources; and*
- *designing a facility to accommodate the overall library program.*

The role of parents in the educational program is another example of an alliance between principals and librarians. On the negative side, budgeting in site-based management affects staffing, and therefore restricts scheduling for the library. Principals must choose how they are going to use their budget for personnel. They may decide that they do not have funds for a professionally certified librarian, and use the funds for a paraprofessional instead. A paraprofessional does not have the credentials to teach, and doesn't have the skills necessary to integrate information literacy skills with curriculum objectives. Nor does the paraprofessional have the training and experience to select books for the library collection. At the same time, the paraprofessional does not have the requisite skills to weed old, outdated titles that are no longer relevant.

Yet another issue related to site-based management is the necessity of providing all teachers with a planning period. Librarians are forced to become part of what is known as the rotation schedule with physical education, art, and music; therefore, teachers and students do not have open access to the library. This rotation plan removes teachers as key players from a library program that is fully integrated into the curriculum. Teachers know the students' interests and abilities and the subject content and therefore are critical members of the library program (AASL Position Statement).

"Superintendents function in the middle of the school operations and are responsible for:

- *leading school reform,*
- *balancing budgets,*
- *hearing personnel cases,*
- *constructing facilities,*
- *negotiating with patrons and colleagues,*
- *communicating with boards, and*
- *responding to the media." (Bosher, 2004)*

"School budgets are 50 percent finance and 50 percent advocacy. Organizational change is part systems and part persuasion. Policy development is the confluence of analysis and argument. Teaching is described as the science of mastering content and the art of marketing instruction. No educational leaders are closer to the grassroots than superintendents and principals. Even with the potential of fallout, when political decisions are being made that affect education, it is absolutely critical for the superintendent to be on the field in the midst of the action" (Bosher, 2004, p. 24).

Librarians need to know about research such as Pat Wilson's concerning the lack of knowledge by administrators of great library programs. The Principal-Preparation programs do not have a school library component (Wilson & Blake, 1993, p. 65).

At the 2000 White House Conference on School Librarians, Gary Hartzell stated, "More than ninety percent of Education Administration professors in a 1999 survey didn't see the principal as an important influence in teacher/librarian collaboration—a notion counter to virtually all research on school site collaboration" (IMLS, 2002). Hartzell writes on the same topic in *School Library Journal*. He states that teachers and administrators are not taught in college prep programs that well-funded school libraries staffed by trained media specialists make a significant difference in student achievement, help teachers do their jobs better, and even enhance administrative practices (Hartzell, 2003, May). They need to see the research in their own professional journals.

Ken Haycock's *Foundations for Effective School Library Media Programs* and Doug Johnson's *The Indispensable Librarian: Surviving (and Thriving) in School Media Centers in the Information Age* provide further enrichment on advocacy by administration. A copy of AASL's "The Principal's Manual" brochure will give your administrator a more thorough understanding of the role of a strong school library (AASL, 2000). *Increasing Academic Achievement through the Library Media Center: A Guide for Teachers,* by David V. Loertscher and Douglas Achterman is an excellent source of information for the administrator.

LSC 6600 School Library Advocacy for Administrators is a short, one-credit graduate course available online from Mansfield University's School Library & Information Technologies Program. Designed as a component of an IMLS (Institute of Museums and Library Service) federal scholarship grant, this online training program for school administrators will increase background knowledge and understandings of the role a quality school library media program plays in the academic success of students. The syllabus lists the program goals for the participants as follows:

- *"Understand the mission and purpose of the school library media program and how a quality, well-supported program can increase student learning.*
- *Increase the knowledge base about collections, access to resources, and evaluation of the school library media program.*
- *Learn leadership attitudes and actions that will help reconceptualize a student-centered, information-powered school library media program and strategies to provide continued support for it" (Kachel, 2005).*

The School of Library & Information Science at Indiana University/Purdue University at Indianapolis offers L553: The School Library Media Specialist as an online course. It focuses on the role of the school library media specialist as an educational leader and center administrator. Emphasis is placed on the evolving role of the teacher librarian as a critical player in the learning community including manager, collaborator, collection and curriculum developer, facilities designer, fiscal agent, planner, advocate, promoter, and evaluator. In addition to building professional knowledge and skills in traditional areas, this course explores accountability, administration, and advocacy aspects of the media specialist's critical leadership role in the learning community. The section on advocacy teaches that a well-developed advocacy program markets, promotes, and rallies people around the mission, issues, and philosophies of your library program. As a result, advocacy must be based on specific needs and supported with evidence (Lamb & Johnson, 2004).

The number one goal across all grade levels in schools is student achievement. School administrators know their very existence depends on how students perform on the tests. Student achievement is a measure of success for all schools. The school librarian is both an ally and asset to principals and administrators who have the difficult job of meeting the goals of state level testing and those in the federal program, No Child Left Behind. The American Association of School Librarians developed and mailed, in November 2004, an informative brochure, "Your School Library Media Program and No Child Left Behind" to administrators. This brochure underscores the importance of forming a partnership with building leaders in meeting the challenges of No Child Left Behind. The following quote is on the front of the brochure: "School library media centers can contribute to improved student achievement by providing instructional materials aligned to the curriculum; by collaborating with teachers, administrators and parents; and by extending their hours of operation beyond the school day" (AASL, 2004).

Lance reports on how school librarians leave no child behind in academic achievement. The No Child Left Behind Act of 2001 updates the Elementary and Secondary Education Act (ESEA). It mandates standards-based testing at the state level and support of research-based strategies for improving academic achievement by students (Lance, 2002).

Credible studies in Colorado, Pennsylvania, Alaska, and Texas prove that schools with good library programs have students who do better academically as measured by standardized test scores. Administrators should therefore devote their resources to improving library programs. Improved library programs do equal improved test scores and more. Administrators work with librarians to help ensure that all students are literate; that all students pass state mandated tests; that all students are technologically literate; that all teachers have the resources and skills necessary to be deemed "highly qualified;" and that all schools remain committed to good educational practices.

Well-stocked and well-staffed libraries do influence the test scores on standardized tests raising them by 10 percent to 20 percent. Lance outlines five roles of an empowered librarian: school leader, program administrator, information and technology facilitator, and collaborative teacher and learner (Lance, 2004).

Effective educational advocacy must address equity, opportunity, quality instruction, and high levels of student achievement. The cornerstones of school library advocacy include collaboration during planning and teaching; access to resources and literacy achievement; effects of administration on library programs; and effects of staffing on the quality of the library program (Asselin, 2002, p. 53).

The recommended philosophy for basing library instruction on the state level (Texas) Essential Knowledge and Skills (TEKS) can be found in the ways librarians support student success in learning and as stated in the Vision and Mission of the School Library Programs: Standards and Guidelines for Texas, May 16, 2005 Revision.

Librarians support student success in learning through the following:

- *Identification of existing library resources (print and electronic) that support curriculum;*
- *Purchase of resources to support the curriculum;*
- *Providing access to library resources for curriculum support;*
- *Alignment of learning objectives of the library's information literacy program with TEKS student expectations;*
- *Collaboration with classroom teachers to design and deliver instruction for curriculum support; and*
- *Design of professional development for administrators, classroom faculty and overall school community (TSLAC, 2005).*

Vision and Mission of Texas School Libraries

"Texas students will attain knowledge and skills to become accomplished readers, independent learners, critical thinkers, creative problem solvers, and informed citizens through the expertise of school librarians and the use of resources and services provided by school library programs" (TSLAC, 2005).

Mission of Texas School Libraries

"The mission of the school library program and school librarian is to ensure that students, teachers, administrators, and staff are effective users of ideas and information.
This mission is accomplished by:

- *Providing intellectual and physical access to materials in all formats;*
- *Providing instruction to foster competence and stimulate interest in reading, viewing, and using information and ideas;*
- *Collaborating with other educators to plan, design, teach, and evaluate information literacy learning experiences to meet the needs of all students; and*
- *Demonstrating effective leadership strategies in the administration of the program and in making connections to the broader learning community" (AASL & AECT, 1998).*

The American Association of School Librarians (AASL) joined the Partnership for 21st Century Skills in June 2004. The Partnership for 21st Century Skills is a leading advocacy organization. It brings together the business community, education leaders, and policymakers to define a powerful vision for 21st century education to ensure every child's success as citizens and workers in the 21st century. A leadership summit entitled "Empowering Learning, Advancing the Profession" took place in March 2005. Library leaders, administrators, reading specialists/researchers, and technology coordinators are taking active roles to cultivate critical thinkers and problems solvers in our schools—students who adopt 21st century skills that focus on mastering information and communication technologies. They will help build strategies and an action plan to address the following challenges:

- *Literacy: Closing the chasm between the reading and library communities.*
- *Student Achievement: Creating and integrating a model enabling librarians to scientifically assess and articulate how they influence student learning.*
- *21st Century Learning Skills/Technology: The librarian will be the prime technology leader and partner in the integration of 21st Century Learning Skills (AASL & Partnership for 21st Century Skills, 2005).*

Advocacy as a Political Activity

Lobbying to win the support of legislators is part of the great democratic tradition. Informed legislative advocates know which lawmakers serve on which committees, and which committees are most important in the legislative process. The voting constituent is significant to the elected official. Other influential people are: campaign donors, civic and business leaders, lobbyists, editors of local media, friends or family members, and others whom they know and trust.

To be effective, library advocates must present themselves as credible, knowledgeable, and articulate. Advocates must have a working knowledge of the political process and their role in it. You can gain support for your library and become a stronger advocate on library issues when you are alert to political activities at the local, state, and national levels. Communication by phone, e-mail, letters, or personal meetings is the key to building good relationships with legislators—not just when library funding comes up for a vote, but on a regular basis. Don't wait for a crisis!

In preparation for the legislative season, the state library association and the association for school librarians through their legislative committees thoroughly study and prioritize the issues to bring us recommendations for consideration during the legislative session.

The Legislative Committee of TLA developed legislative requests in 2005 as follows:

- *Good school libraries equal higher student achievement. A study sponsored by the Texas State Library and Archives Commission demonstrated that over 10 percent more students in schools with librarians than in schools without librarians met minimum reading expectations in standardized assessment tests.*
- *School libraries are a vital instructional component of education in the K-12 learning environment, and school librarians are essential information managers, instructors of the Texas Essential Knowledge and Skills (TEKS), and teaching partners working to provide Texas children with the highest quality education.*

- *School librarians are frontline educational professionals who spend, on average, 75 percent of their time teaching students and faculty how to locate, evaluate, and use information and have, by certification standards, classroom teaching experience.*

- *State support for school libraries is minimal. The Texas Education Agency offers no specified support for school library programs or school librarians, despite the personal commitment of curriculum staff to help foster school library development. At this time, Education Service Centers throughout Texas are the primary means of support for school library programs.*

- *Providing a strong, broad-based education involves supporting school libraries, which support both specific curriculum tasks and lifelong learning. For example, approximately 60 percent of TEKS [Texas Essential Knowledge and Skills] are process-based skills and are taught in the school library. In fact, the Texas Standards for School Libraries are linked to key areas of the TEKS.*

Recommended actions include the following:

- *Support legislation which specifies that library and media programs should be categorized as instructional under state definitions in Chapter 44 of the Education Code.*
- *Support reauthorization of the Education Service Centers.*
- *Contact TEA about agency support for school library programs (TLA Legislative Committee, 2005).*

The legislative agenda gains strength when all types of libraries work together for the good of the whole. Library advocates must be able to articulate issues in a way that transcends partisan politics, acknowledges economic realities, and positions libraries as part of the solution to larger problems.

Face-to face discussion is the most effective means of communication and helps to establish a solid working relationship. Legislative Day for Librarians is planned down to the last detail, and provides librarians with opportunities to meet with their legislators. The legislative requests must be well articulated in a simple and straight forward way with facts and figures, and the impact the requested legislation will have on the use of libraries by the students and the public. On the flip side, it is important that the legislators know the losses, as well as the gains if a request isn't funded. Bring a policy statement or fact sheets that supports your position. The information has been condensed to provide the legislator with the most pertinent facts.

One of the major goals for Legislative Day is that library constituents from all legislative districts are present. Appointments are made with the legislators, and the lobby day participants wear name badges to help the legislator know they are talking with a librarian from their district. Nothing speaks louder than having a voting constituents meet with their representative or senator. Librarians are trained on the legislative issues, and they are trained about the political process. When the request is introduced as a bill, librarians know that it is important to write or speak to the chairs of specified legislative committees and to the members of that committee. The bills go through a hearing process, and library leaders testify about the importance of the bill. As the bill moves forward to the floor of the House or the Senate, all legislators who have been contacted by their voting constituent are more likely to support the bill.

There are many ways to communicate with legislators. Some make it easy by providing a link on their Web sites. Most prefer letters or visits. Listservs are very important avenues of communicating to the librarians within each of their types of libraries about key library issues. The postings alert them to write their legislators. They are encouraged to look for the latest updates on library legislative news, and subscribe to a free e-mail publication that will be sent to members of the listserv whenever important library news is breaking. Communication with the appropriate legislators is guided by the content of the notices.

Turning legislators into champions for libraries takes more than a single visit. Make time to develop a relationship—one based on trust, respect, and positive feelings. Look for opportunities to make both them—and you—look good. Anything you can do to help them will be appreciated—and remembered. Remember to thank the legislators in person, in writing, and in public. Let them know how much you appreciate their support of libraries in multiple ways.

Carol Brey-Casiano, the 2005 ALA president from Texas witnessed successful advocacy-in-action when the commissioners voted to close because of a budget crisis in the only public library outside of the El Paso city limits. This act gave her renewed enthusiasm for her presidential initiative to create a grassroots advocacy campaign that encourages every citizen to "Stand Up and Speak Out for Libraries." It is just as important to garner long-term support that will ensure the library's existence for many future generations.

Yet another ALA President, Patricia Glass Shuman, speaks up about the need for library advocates to maintain round-the-clock passion about access and equity and a spirit that doesn't accept defeat. Her 10-point checklist emphasizes the importance of membership and involvement in professional associations, advocacy training, legislative participation, and visibility (Shuman, 1999, p. 50).

At the national level, congressional members must be helped to understand the role of libraries and librarians in the electronic age. They must understand:

- *The importance of federal and state leadership in library funding.*
- *The significance of libraries when dealing with intellectual property, confidentiality, freedom of information, and other policy issues.*
- *The relative modest investment of tax dollars that result in huge benefits.*

The American Library Association's key points on libraries include:

- *"Libraries are central to a literate society.*
- *Libraries help prepare Americans of all ages to compete in a global economy.*
- *Libraries are "wired." They make information technology available to all.*
- *Public libraries are community assets. They are resource centers for education, employment, and recreation.*
- *Libraries are part of the American dream. They are a place for education and self-help.*
- *Libraries bring opportunity to all—including poor, minority, immigrant, and rural populations.*
- *School libraries play a crucial role in preparing youth to be literate, productive citizens.*
- *Academic libraries are critical to advancing knowledge"* (ALA Issues & Advocacy).

Advocacy Tools from Associations and Organizations

The Friends of School Libraries, Volunteers in Public Schools, Parent/Teacher Organizations, and professional library associations at the state and national levels are most supportive of libraries. Professional organizations epitomize the meaning of advocacy. Through their publications, communication, conference programming, annual assembly for the working groups within the executive board, committees, divisions, round tables, and library districts, the professional library association provides the leadership and addresses the key issues in libraries at the local, district, regional, and state level. The state organizations mirror many of the activities at the national level.

The American Library Association and the American Association of School Librarians provide lenses to view and use their professional tools and publications in building libraries that serve the educational needs of students. "ALA strives to communicate the importance of libraries and librarians to our democratic society, to improve library funding and influence public policy about libraries and information-related issues, to increase public awareness about the role and importance of libraries and library workers in every community, and ultimately, to turn passive support of libraries and librarians into educated action by stakeholders" (ALA Advocacy for Libraries, 2005).

The Online Advocacy Action Kit at <www.ala.org/advocacyactionkit> is a collection of existing ALA advocacy materials, compiled into one online location. The kit includes tips for talking to legislators, the public and the media, how to mount an advocacy campaign, and online resources for advocates. The action kit is titled "Stand Up and Speak Out" under the training umbrella of Library Advocacy Now @ Your Library™. You will find tips and strategies to help you garner the support you need to promote your library program to students, teachers, and administrators.

Friends of Libraries, U.S.A. has developed fact sheets for advocates. There is no reason to re-invent the wheel. You have a vast arsenal of information available to you on the Web. The process takes you from A to Z. You can use their messages, tips, and strategies. Their questions will guide you along the pathway to success.

While Friends of Libraries, U.S.A. is an excellent ally states must also organize and act. Friends of School Libraries in Texas advocate and promote school libraries locally throughout the state of Texas. They foster the development and growth of local groups in support of their own school libraries. They advocate and raise funds for school library programs and resources. Friends include local business and community members, parents, students, and anyone who desires to promote a love of reading and the importance of communication of information. Participation will increase students' ability to explore, discover, and learn because school libraries are where students become effective users of ideas and information (TLA, 2005).

Advocacy as a Role within a Campus Setting

The library of yesteryear where you met your friends to have lunch or study, where you came to get out of class or even skip class, or where you came to conduct research for that dreaded research assignment in English looks and acts differently in today's environment. Enter and find a new and exciting place where information is available in a wide variety of formats, both print and electronic; where materials and activities are coordinated with classroom assignments; and where students learn information skills that will prepare them to live and work in the 21st century.

Today's school library media program plays an integral role in educating youth for the future. It is where students learn to find, analyze, evaluate, interpret, and communicate information and ideas—skills they will need as adults to live and work in an information-based society. An emerging definition is that libraries are in the knowledge business. In addition to serving as independent learning centers, the programs of many libraries are directly integrated into the curriculum objectives.

Texas has bragging rights on the selection of Northside Independent School District in San Antonio, Texas as the winner of the National School Library Media Award. It is sponsored by the American Association of School Librarians and Follett Library Resources. This prestigious award honors school districts and individual schools for demonstrating excellence in school library media programs, which ensure that students and staff are effective users of ideas and information, and exemplify the implementation of Information Power. Superintendent Dr. John N. Folks said in his letter of support: "In the NISD libraries, the 'labs of lifelong learning,' Northside's students can learn and grow and become tomorrow's leaders in a democratic society." All NISD libraries are staffed with certified librarians and full-time library assistants and each librarian partners with the computer integration teacher. The district's library coordinator, Jana Knezek, assures that staff development is available for library media specialists, faculty, and administration. The librarians work with Jana and her staff to deliver staff development in an ongoing way. They acknowledged that looking at their program from a different perspective helped them win (AASL, 2004 & Knezek, 2005).

First Lady Laura Bush hosted on June 4, 2002 the first-ever White House conference on school libraries, spotlighting research that ties academic achievement to strong school library programs. "Libraries allow children to ask questions about the world and find answers. And the wonderful thing is that once a child learns to use a library, the doors to learning are always open," noted the First Lady, who was once a school librarian (Bush, 2002). Mrs. Bush was joined by education, library, government, and philanthropic leaders from across the country. In his keynote address Dr. Vartan Gregorian, Carnegie Corporation, stated: "Through the development and spread of the academic and private libraries, and the central role that our public libraries and school libraries have assumed, we have come to view the library not only as a source of scholarship, knowledge and learning, but also as a medium for self-education, progress, self-help, autonomy, liberation, empowerment, self-determination and 'moral salvation' as a source of power. That is why the library was dubbed the 'People's University' by Emerson, and the 'True University' or the 'House of Intellect' by Carlyle" (IMLS, 2002).

The role model for library advocacy in the campus setting is the school librarian. Librarians support 60 percent of the curriculum objectives covered in the standardized tests. Studies have shown that schools with professional librarians have 10 percent more students passing the state achievement tests. Encouraging reading is still an important component of their job, but more important is teaching students how to do research, even at the elementary level. They don't have to wait until they reach high school. You can witness real learning and achievement when the elementary librarian conducts major research projects for second and third graders, in collaboration with the classroom teachers. These young children are guided in the proper techniques of ferreting out and evaluating information (Penny, 2004, 4A).

Raising Student Achievement through Texas School Libraries is a dissertation written by Marybeth Green. It concerns the librarian's collaboration with the teachers to create a Texas Assessment of Knowledge and Skills (TAKS) Support Plan. The librarian collaborates with teachers in a specific discipline, such as math or reading, to review and analyze the test results and determine a plan of action with selected resources to remediate targeted curriculum skills. The tutorials build knowledge, understanding, and critical thinking skills. The ultimate goal for the students is to improve their overall score on the next test scores and specifically in the targeted areas. The TAKS Support Plan is a model partnership among teachers and librarians to work on specified areas of the TAKS tests where student performance revealed lack of understanding and to build a plan with resources to gain understanding. The major focus is "Helping Teachers Teach." Dr. Phil Turner at the University of North Texas said, "Consider how many students you are able to impact when you impact a single teacher."

Budget planning and preparation are important campus level responsibilities. The budget process may begin as early as November, so plan to have a 30 minute sit-down meeting with your principal sometime in late fall.

> *1) First, determine your principal's priorities. Usually student achievement is number one.*
>
> *2) Analyze your library, library program, library resources, and your own strengths and weaknesses. Determine what areas need to be bolstered by next year's budget.*
>
> *3) Consider the district goals, the Portrait of the Graduate, and the Superintendent's Parameters as you look for ways the library program can support the school.*
>
> *4) Prepare to highlight the library program needs that could assist in accomplishing the principal's priorities. Make specific proposals.*
>
> *5) Use published research of library studies to make your points about the library's role in student achievement.*
>
> *6) When meeting with the principal, stay positive. Point out how he or she can be more successful at accomplishing his or her goals on the state's standardized tests by supporting your proposed library budget and plan (Bishop, 2005).*

The school library budget must be prepared at the building level and at the district level. The largest percentage of a school budget goes for personnel. As library leaders, you must know about the budget process. You will find Doug Johnson's (2005) "Strategies for Assisting Library Media Specialists Whose Positions Are in Jeopardy" a helpful resource in working with your overall budget. His guidelines address the jobs of librarians that might be on the line because of budget shortfalls. He clearly states the need to be proactive with library advocacy information before the ax falls. He also advises the librarians to perform at the highest possible level. He goes on to list twelve activities to keep the budget wolf away from the door. They reflect a strong library program serving the needs of educators through instructional collaboration with documented proof of the impact on student learning and achievement.

> *1) "Build and maintain a library program that teaches information and technology literacy skills, builds literacy rates, and supports all classrooms and curriculum.*
>
> *2) Serve the needs of your teaching and administrative staff through instructional collaboration.*
>
> *3) Establish a school library advisory board composed of parents, students, and teachers.*
>
> *4) Create long-term goals tied directly to the building's goals.*
>
> *5) Build a mutually supportive relationship with your principal.*
>
> *6) Track and report what is going on in the school library in terms of units of teaching, collaboration, and specific skills you teach.*
>
> *7) Communicate regularly and formally with administrators, teachers, students, parents, and the community about what happens in the library program.*
>
> *8) Be involved with the parent organization in your school.*
>
> *9) Serve on leadership, curriculum, technology, and staff development teams in your building and district.*
>
> *10) Be active in your professional organization.*
>
> *11) Be involved in extracurricular life of the school.*
>
> *12) Be active in your state school library association" (Johnson, 2005, p. 44).*

Advocacy as a Role within a Community Setting

If you are conducting a large-scale advocacy initiative, you will need to reach out to people at the grassroots level and encourage them to voice their views to legislators or decision-makers, to vote, to give money, or to provide other support. The selected strategies discussed next were developed by AASL committees and can help to focus public attention and generate support.

Speaking engagements are an excellent way to tell the library's story and to build relationships with other organizations. They say, "A picture is worth a thousand words." Pictures of a library overflowing with enthusiastic kids, very few books on the shelves, and teachers and librarians working with students, convey a powerful message.

Preparation, practice, and passion will gain the attention of the audience. Special events such as Children's Book Week can be designed to take the library message outside the library or to bring key audiences, such as legislators, parents, or business owners, into the library. Use national library and literacy events, such as Children's Book Week or National Library Week, National Poetry Month, Teen Read Week in October, Read across America, National Book Month, American Education Week, and other events to help generate publicity for your library. Visit <www.ala.org/pio> and click on Calendar for specific dates of these important events. Rallies are colorful events designed to attract the media and focus public attention on your message (ALA Library Promotional Events & Available PIO Materials, 2005).

"Word of mouth is more than just telling people. It's delivering a consistent message and getting those people to tell other people. Think of the possibilities. Millions of people walk through library doors each day. But how often have we said to them, "Please tell your friends." Creative librarians call it planting an "idea virus." We need people to be talking up libraries the same way Harley riders talk about their bikes. Some call this talk the walk.

> *"Have a simple message that is easy to say and deliver.*
>
> *Challenge yourself to talk to five people a day about the library and ask them to spread the word.*
>
> *Deliver the message in a way that makes people feel—not just think— that the library is important. Have fun. Let your passion show!"*
> *(AASL Action Kit, 2005)*

Print communications continue to be a primary source of information. Editorial endorsements from influential newspapers can be powerful with officials and voters. You have the opportunity to make the case for support and to answer questions. Feature stories are generally longer than news stories and can explore an issue in more depth, or they might profile noteworthy people. Writing a letter to the editor is an easy way to show your support. Most newspapers carry letters to the editor as a way for their readers to voice their views on items in the news. If the library doesn't receive adequate funding, you may ask members of the board or Friends to write letters expressing their concern.

The Library Advocate's Checklist can be accessed under "Stand Up and Speak for American Libraries." "Each of us has countless opportunities to speak out for libraries in our daily lives. Speaking out now will strengthen today's libraries and help to ensure free and open access to information for future generations" (AASL, Advocacy Toolkit).

Formation of Friends Group

If athletic teams and bands have their boosters, why shouldn't your library have a Friends group? Many public, school, and academic libraries have discovered the advantages of having a Friends group to assist with fund raising, provide volunteer assistance, and advocate support. It is also a good way to nurture a core group of advocates in good times, as well as bad.

Friends of Libraries USA, a national organization provides support to local Friends groups, and offers the following advice for organizing a Friends of School Libraries.

- *Determine the purpose of the group.*
- *Identify and develop a core of leaders, who will work closely with library administrators.*
- *Acquaint the Friends with the basic philosophy and requirements for an effective library. Define organizational structure, dues structure.*
- *Plan an orientation program/welcome event for new members. Explain policies and procedures, pertinent state and national standards.*
- *Develop a membership recruitment campaign with strategies for reaching out to potential members.*
- *Keep records and periodically evaluate the program.*
- *Recognize and thank your Friends and volunteers (FOLUSA Brochure, 2005).*

Advocacy with Other Types of Educational Institutions

School libraries reap immense benefits from advocacy with public libraries, community colleges, and colleges and universities. All librarians are stronger because they work together to achieve their purposes and goals through their involvement in state library associations. "The Power and Promise of Partnerships" examines the need to enter into partnerships for the common good of libraries and their constituents. Answers to the how, why, and what of partnerships provide a framework for building. The collaborative process comes in the form of advocacy, alliances, cooperation, fund raising, and various other potential ways (Moore, 2001, p. 8).

The legislative agenda is a premier example of advocating for public libraries that serve all the people, all the time from birth to life. At institutions of learning, students move through their preschool years in the public library, to public schools for their pre-K-12 education, to community colleges and colleges and universities, and then into their professions and retirement. Libraries are for life.

Advocacy for School Libraries by State Libraries

Advocacy for school libraries by state libraries can be powerful. One example of this advocacy took place in a Texas study, which is discussed in the following section. Use this example as a possible model to begin advocacy in your own state.

To begin this advocacy effort, Mary Lankford, the Director of Library Media Services at the Texas Education Agency (TEA), initiated a dialogue with Peggy Rudd, the Texas State Librarian at the Texas State Libraries & Archives Commission (TSLAC). They knew that research in Colorado, Alaska, and Pennsylvania had focused attention on the role of librarians and libraries in student achievement. Because a need for revising the "Texas School Library Programs: Standards and Guidelines for Texas" had been identified, the two agencies initiated a study in Texas to correlate student achievement with school library standards implementation. The study, *"Texas School Libraries: Standards, Resources, Services, and Students' Performance"* was designed to provide support for updating the standards.

The TSLAC contracted with EGS Research and Consulting of Austin to conduct the study, which was completed in April 2001. The full study report was published by the Texas State Libraries & Archives Commission and is available on the TSL Web site at <www.tsl.state.tx.us/ld/pubs/schlibsurvey/index.html>. The study provides solid, systematic data on the contributions of libraries and librarians. Some pertinent points on Texas school libraries are as follows:

- *One-quarter of the schools in Texas do not have librarians.*
- *Schools without librarians are lower performing on standardized tests than schools with librarians. On average, 10 percent more students in schools with librarians met minimum expectations in reading than in schools without librarians.*
- *Librarian activities that have impact on student performance include planning and teaching collaboratively with teachers and training teachers. In schools with librarians and supporting staff, teachers spend more time collaborating.*
- *No collaboration takes place in schools with one librarian.*
- *In libraries staffed with one aide, no collaborative activities take place because the aide isn't certified.*
- *Increased library use is the result of adequate staffing.*
- *The greatest impact on student performance takes place when the library is staffed with a minimum of a professional librarian and aide.*
- *The growing presence of networked resources has increased the importance of the librarian's training role with regard to the integration of technology resources into the curriculum (McNew & Lankford, 2001, p. 48).*

The result of this study and findings was the *2005 School Library Programs: Standards and Guidelines for Texas*. In accordance with Texas Education Code § 33.021, the TSLAC, in consultation with the State Board of Education, adopted standards for school library services on March 19, 2004. Staff at the TEA reviewed the revised Standards and Guidelines and recommended changes. The State Board of Education signed a Resolution of Support for the revised Standards and Guidelines, with changes recommended by TEA staff, at their November 2004 meeting.

The standards, revised and adopted on March 19, 2004, and again on May 16, 2005, establish guidelines for school library programs at four levels: exemplary, recognized, acceptable, and below standard. They include output and outcome measures that libraries may use to describe the level of use and effectiveness of the program.

Advocacy Action Plan

An advocacy action plan requires you to look carefully at your overall library program, literacy, student achievement, 21st century learning skills and technology, marketing, author visits, collection development, staffing, volunteers, equipment, hardware, and software. Every public school student deserves a school library with open access and flexible scheduling, relevant and current books, in an attractive welcoming facility staffed by a certified school librarian with assistance. Maintaining or increasing funding, lobbying for state legislation, fundraising, and grant writing give you the financial tools necessary to accomplish your goals. After you target five key issues, you will prioritize the list and set your goals.

Repeat the number one library advocacy goal over and over in news releases, letters to the editor, and other communications. You might even translate the statement into an advertising slogan. Think about the feelings of compassion, concern, anger, or joy that you want to ignite in others.

In addition to school administrators and other key decision makers, think about other groups you would like to reach with your message. The faculty and the library volunteers will under gird the need for a professionally certified librarian in all schools. Why are your issues important to them? Literacy, student achievement, the integration of technology and learning skills into the curriculum, and the equity of staffing all schools with a professionally certified librarian are education issues with links to the mission of the school library. You build a case for each of the issues when you list three supporting points:

> *1) A professionally certified librarian is an essential member of the teaching and learning team.*
>
> *2) Reading is the very foundation of learning. Literate students are successful in their school assignments and when testing for achievement. IRA members are concerned about having a strong and positive impact on education policy. Over the years IRA has issued numerous position statements and policy advisories on topics such as school libraries, access to quality teaching and learning materials, high-stakes testing, government mandates, the role of phonics in reading instruction, and the importance of excellent teachers.*
>
> *3) Students are motivated learners when they use library resources as an integral part of the curriculum.*

The most important thing you want others to know is the Formula for Learning.

> **Formula for Learning**
>
> *Master Teachers + Dynamic Librarians + Curriculum Integration = Student Achievement and Motivated, Lifelong Learners.*

Librarians engage students in reading, writing, and research. They develop analytical thinking and reading comprehension—necessary building blocks of education. School librarians expand student horizons. School administrators know that kids who like to read, read more and read better. Stephen Krashen (1993) writes that reading is the primary indicator of academic success. To learn to read, one must practice. Dr. Krashen (1993) lists proven facts about the connection between school libraries and reading success:

- *"Access to school library media centers results in more voluntary reading by students.*
- *Having a school library media specialist makes a difference in the amount of voluntary reading done.*
- *Larger school library collections and longer hours increase both the circulation and amount read.*
- *When books are readily available, more reading is done.*
- *Second-language learners are more successful in language acquisition when they read more in the second language"* (p. 34-39).

Researcher Keith Lance has proven once again that libraries improve student learning. Lance's study in New Mexico with fellow researchers Marcia Rodney and Christine Hamilton-Pennel (as cited in Whelan, 2003) found that no matter how poor a school library program, "incremental improvements in staffing, collections, and funding will yield incremental increases in reading scores" (p. 68).

Advocacy, a Story with Demonstrated Results

Parents are very important members of a student's learning experience. They offer unique insight and can be important allies in the advocacy effort because they have the opportunities to see and hear changes in their child's school experiences that teachers and librarians might not be able to recognize. They especially know how to compare and contrast learning experiences when they move from a district with superior school libraries where every library is staffed with a professional librarian to a district with acceptable or below standard ratings where three out of 10 libraries are not staffed with professional librarians. After all, school librarians are key figures in teaching and learning, literacy, curriculum integration, and technology applications in districts with exemplary and recognized ratings.

Parents can also detect a change in their children's enthusiasm for learning. They obviously become concerned when their child has declining grades and less interest in school. They can see first-hand the impact a strong librarian, teamed with a strong teacher, can have on a student. Following is an advocacy story with demonstrated results!

One day a mother noticed her son was reading more than she ever imagined him reading, and more importantly, her son wanted to read. Reading opened up an entirely new world for her son, and she noticed he also began to develop a relationship with the librarian on his campus. Her son trusted the librarian to help him make good choices when selecting books in his area of interest. And when the librarian suggested a book, and he read it and loved it, the mother thought this reinforced further the life-long impact the librarian would have on him. The parents celebrated their son's victory with reading and became confident that he was being given the tools he needed to become a life-long learner.

The library experience for this family's younger son was in stark contrast. He had already spent his first two years (kindergarten and first grade) in a school without a librarian. He would not have the benefit of being a student in a school with a library run by a full-time, certified librarian until Fourth grade. This reality became a large concern to the mother and motivated her to become proactive about professional staffing at her children's schools.
As the concerned mother contemplated what to do, she thought about what she already knew. She knew that she definitely saw a difference in the older son's performance when he began attending a school with a certified librarian. She also knew that a certified librarian ran a library differently than an aide did. She knew this because, as a volunteer in both libraries, she witnessed first-hand on a regular basis that difference; and the difference was enormous—from the interaction with the students, which to her was the biggest indicator, to the ability to work with teachers and volunteers. After thinking this through, she decided she needed to act.

At the point the mother decided to act, she moved to the information stage of the advocacy process. The mother formed a parent advocate group and remembered a quote from an Eighth grade teacher, which she had committed to memory, "Once you have learned to ask questions, relevant, substantial, and appropriate questions, you have learned how to learn, and no one can keep you from learning whatever it is you want or need to know." The parent advocates took this advice to heart and started their advocacy effort. They knew that librarians were an important part of all children's education. At this point, they didn't have any idea why libraries were important to the reading and learning process, or how to articulate it in a way that made a difference to those who made such decisions.

After meeting with the principal, the parent advocates began calling all of the school board members. The board members were responsive, and they were not aware of the importance of staffing school libraries with professionally certified librarians. It became very apparent that the issue of library staffing in the district had not been raised during the board's tenure. The issue had been raised with the superintendent and the assistant superintendents, but it had not been taken to the school board, because school board members rely on school administrators to raise such issues. Board members asked why professional librarians were important to their children's education. The parent advocates received insight into how things worked at the board and district level, as well as what questions needed answers for them to show the importance of properly trained librarians in all schools. In fact, one board member said that in this time of budget cutting, it was insane to ask about adding staff. The board member stated clearly that the parent advocates needed to prove that the value of full-time certified librarians on all campuses exceeded the value of other staff and programs that were being considered for cuts.

After meeting with the school board, the parent advocates knew they needed to broaden the scope of their mission. In order to be taken seriously, they understood that they needed to become advocates for all of the campuses in the district that were inadequately staffed.

When the quest was expanded, the parent advocates realized it was important to come up with a library staffing history for the district to show that professional librarians had not been added even when the district was not in a budget crisis. They achieved this goal with the cooperation of many long-time librarians some of whom were even retired. The one-page history prevented district administrators and school board members from saying, "We can't staff librarians—we just don't have the money." The bleak history of inadequate staffing within the district was there in black and white, and there was no way that it could be argued that it was due to a "lack of funds" or that it was "the state legislature's" fault. Rather it was very clear that adequately and equitably staffing these school libraries had never been a priority in the district. Three schools went 19, 16, and 15 years without the service of a full-time certified librarian, while others were staffed with a librarian. Funding was not a problem in the district during that time; the district simply had not considered it a priority to staff these three schools with professional librarians.

After developing the staffing history, the parent advocates spoke with the state agency professionals and the library development professional at the state library. They were directed to many Web sites and individuals who could help. They scheduled a meeting with the district's lead librarian to ask questions about critical information found in School Library Standards and the Southern Association of Colleges and Schools. They learned the history of what the school librarians had done to push for certified librarians in the three schools who did not have the services of full-time librarians. The lead librarian gathered information on collection size, circulation numbers, and serial and Internet subscriptions from all school libraries in the district. A retired school librarian helped make sense of the data and how to apply it to the state library guidelines and standards.

The parents and the volunteer groups in the school were encouraged to form a Friends of School Libraries group by the lead librarian. The time had come for organized voices from outside the local group of librarians. The lead librarian remained involved as a guide. The parent advocates were involved in their mission and very conscious of a tight timeline for the budgeting process. To avoid the cart before the horse plan, the Friends group organized first. The Friends formed a Coordinating Committee to ensure that their advocacy efforts became a reality. A chair was selected. Committees were then established. One person assumed responsibility for contacting and recruiting members. A calendar was developed for committee meetings. The CC kept track of the project, set deadlines for the tasks, and delegated specific tasks. Groups and individuals on the team included parents, volunteers in school libraries, Friends of School Libraries, librarians, principals in the affected campuses, the superintendent, board of education, and the entire community, through the feature stories and editorial pages in the newspaper (Jimenez, 2004, p. 1A & Duncan, 2004, p. 4A).

In the meantime, the parent advocates' crusade for full-time professionally certified libraries continued. They read and reviewed the Standards for School Libraries in Texas, both the 1995 edition and the Revised Standards for School Libraries in Texas, 2001-2005. The number one Principle for Staffing was that the librarian manages staff, volunteers, and partners to support the curriculum, to satisfy learners' diverse needs, and to encourage lifelong learning. The parent advocates summarized the information they pulled from the Standards for purposes of the role of school librarians in education. They researched the Southern Association of Colleges and Schools and noted that the staffing recommendations made in the report are extremely minimal. They learned that in schools with enrollment of 264 or greater, a library program run by anyone other than a full-time certified librarian is considered inadequately staffed. The district's lead librarian directed the advocates' attention to studies from Texas and Colorado that showed a correlation between school library resources and services and greater student achievement. The Texas study in 2001 found that an increase in the library budget, an increase in the appropriate level of library staff, and an increase in the time library staff members spend with students and faculty will increase academic performance of students.

The district information office, as well as the district business manager, dutifully gave the parent advocates the requested information so they could measure not only the district according to the Guidelines, but also each individual campus as well. Although they did not have these measures finalized by the time they met with the superintendent, they did have a general idea that many schools fell "Below Standard" in many areas.

Before the lead parent advocate scheduled meetings with the principals of the schools without librarians, she pulled together a concise but comprehensive report of her findings. She wanted to be completely clear about the facts and her understanding of the Standards. She conferred with Christine McNew with the Texas State Library and Mary Lankford with the Library Division at the Texas Education Agency since McNew and Lankford were responsible for oversight of the Standards.

Who did the advocates meet with at this point? With site-based management, they scheduled meetings with each of the building level principals. After meeting with the principals, the parent advocates found that while the principals supported the theory and value of certified librarians in their school libraries, they couldn't financially support the recommendation. One of the principals suggested moving up the ladder to a meeting with the school superintendent.

The lead parent advocate presented the concerns and facts to the superintendent in clear and concise terms. She asked about the equity of the decision to staff only seven of the 10 libraries in the district. She underscored the difference in school performance and achievement. She told him about the difference in motivation for learning when the school has a dynamic library program. The superintendent listened and empathized with the concerns of the parents in the schools without certified librarians. He went on to say that the district just did not have the budget to fund the request for certified librarians in the three schools. The parent advocate then indicated that she would be requesting a place on the Board agenda to speak to them about her findings and request their support of a full-time certified librarian devoted solely to each school. She told the superintendent that the group planned to write letters to the editor of the local newspaper. She told him they would be asking for a feature article in the local newspaper during National Library Week. When the superintendent realized the Friends were organized, informed, and determined, he scheduled the parent advocates to speak to the board. They had done their homework, and they developed a well-documented plan.

The parent advocates compiled a tabbed notebook for each board member with reference points as they presented a very solid case with the facts and figures that each school in the district must have full-time professionally certified librarians. They had used the School Library Standards and Guidelines to measure where each of the schools in the district stood with staffing, collections, technology, literacy, research, and curriculum.

As a result of their very thorough research into the educational justifications for certified school librarians, their concern for equity in staffing each school library with certified librarians, and their role in supporting 60 percent of the essential elements that are covered in standardized testing, the three positions were listed in the budget proposals for the 2005 school year. The recommendation made all the budget hurdles, and the three libraries were staffed with full-time certified librarians for the first time ever in the history of the schools. Feedback from the principal of one of the newly staffed libraries indicated that he now has a clear vision of the distinctive differences between a professionally certified librarian and a clerk. He noted that the certified librarian is:

- *a literary resource for the classroom teachers;*
- *a professional with views of the strengths and weaknesses of the current collection;*
- *a systematic trainer of students in the area of library skills;*
- *a leader in school technology initiatives;*
- *a coordinator of parent volunteers in the library; and*
- *an additional tutor for reading programs.*

Now that every school library is staffed with a professionally certified librarian, will everyone live happily ever after? Can the Friends sit back and gloat about their successes? No, there is more work to do.

- *They must continue to tell their story on the speaker circuit. They were invited to speak at the Texas Library Association 2005 Conference in Austin, Texas. They prepared a powerful "How To" document of their step-by-step journey (Duncan & Hardwick, 2005, p. 1-8).*

- *The teachers must learn how to work with the librarian. They are not accustomed to a certified librarian on their team, who is involved in the teaching of the essential knowledge and skills for the curriculum and who serves as the information coach for students and teachers. The top 10 reasons a librarian is a teacher's best friend comes with collaboration beginning with improving test scores, improved teaching, copyright and fair use, selection and use of information, knowledge of the curriculum and resources and technology, and equal access (Hylen, 2004, p. 219).*

- *The library collections in the schools are not up to par. Selecting current relevant, meaningful, and interesting library materials requires a real connection among students, teachers, and the curriculum objectives. As the Friends contemplate fund raising to buy books for the libraries, they can consider the many potential grant opportunities.*

- *They must keep a vision or a goal in front of them. When there is a gap in working toward the goals, tasks can be moved to other individuals.*
- *Some members suffer from burnout and dropout problems. Including teachers and more parents can strengthen the network. Without question, more parents are needed to carry the banner and become more involved in the work at hand. The front lines should be reinforced with new members.*
- *Teachers are helpful allies in the advocacy process.*

Conclusion

The previous story was just one success story in school library advocacy. There are many others and many advocacy efforts just beginning. School libraries need strong advocate groups and advocacy efforts as education dollars are stretched to cover many areas and issues. As shown in this chapter, school libraries have the benefit of professional studies and statistics to back up their importance as well as allies in administrators, teachers, parents, and the overall community. Advocacy is "an ongoing plan to develop support and understanding through specific and sustained efforts over time incrementally" (Haycock, 1990, n.p.). Keep up the good work!

Works Cited

American Association of School Librarians. *AASL Advocacy Toolkit*. 16 June 2005 http://www.ala.org/aasl/advocacy.

American Association of School Librarians. (2000). *The principal's manual for your school library media program*. Chicago: AASL.

American Association of School Librarians. (2004). *Your school library media program and No Child Left Behind*. Retrieved, Dec. 10, 2005 from http://www.ala.org/ala/aaslbucket/aaslnclbbrochure.htm

American Association of School Librarians, & Association for Educational Communications and Technology. (1998). *Information power: Building partnerships for learning*. Chicago: ALA.

American Association of School Librarians, & Partnership for 21st Century Skills. Empowering learners, advancing the profession. (2005). *21st Century Skills. 2005 Leadership Summit*. Chicago: ALA and School Library Journal.

American Library Association. (2005). *Action Kit*. 18 June 2005 http://www.ala.org/Template.cfm?Section=actionkit&Template=/MembersOnly.cfm7NavMenuID=5787&ContentKD-92642&DuirectListComboInd=D

American Library Association. 2005. *Advocacy for Libraries*. 18 June 2005 http://www.ala.org/aasltemplate.cfm?Section=aaslissues.

American Library Assoication. 2005. *Issues and Advocacy*. 18 June 2005 http://www.ala.org/aasltemplate.cfm?Section=aaslissues.

American Library Association. (2005). *Library advocacy now*. Chicago: ALA.

American Library Association. (2005). *Library Promotional Events*. 18 June 2005 http://www.ala.org/ala/aasl/conferencesandevents/librarypromoevents/librarypormotional.htm.

Asselin, M. (2002, Oct.). Evidence-based practice. *Teacher Librarian,* 30.1, 53-54. Professional Development Collection. EBSCO. New Braunfels Pub. Lib. New Braunfels, TX. Retrieved June 14, 2005 from http://search.epnet.com/login.aspx?direct=true&db=tfh&an=8523949

Bishop, B. (2005). Advocacy & leadership for libraries. *Spring Branch ISD Texas: Library Information Services Web Site*. Hill Country Librarians Conf. Spring Branch, TX: Spring Branch Library Information Services. Technology and Learning: The Advocacy Advantage. Retrieved June 14, 2005 from http://library.springbranchisd.com

Bosher, W. C., Jr. (2004, Mar.). A game plan: Superintendents on the field of advocacy. School Administrator, 61.3, 24-25. Professional Development Collection. EBSCO. New Braunfels Pub. Lib. New Braunfels, TX. Retrieved June 14, 2005 from http://search.epnet.com/login.aspx?direct=true&db=tfh&an=12350557

Brey-Casiano, C. (2004, Nov.). President's message. *American Libraries,* 35.10, 5.

Bush, L., First Lady. (2002). Interview. White House Conference on School Libraries: Proceedings. Washington, DC: IMLS.

Duncan, E. (2004, April 13). Every school should have a full-time, certified librarian. *Herald–Zeitung*, p. 4A.

Duncan, E., & Hardwick, S. (2005). Parents speak for school librarians. Texas Association of School Library Administrators. Texas Library Association Annual Conf. Austin, TX: TASLA, 1-8.

Friends of Libraries U.S.A. Your school library media center has a friend when you join FOLUSA. Philadelphia, PA: Friends of Libraries U.S.A., 2004.

Funding Texas libraries. (2005, Mar. 11). *The Houston Chronicle,* Editorial.

Green, M. (2005). *Raising student achievement through Texas school libraries.* Dissertation, Texas A&M University, College Station, TX.

Hartzell, G. (2003, February). Ready ... aim ... aim again. *School Library Journal,* 49.2, 41.

Hartzell, G. (2003, May). A show of strength. *School Library Journal,* 49.5, 45.

Hartzell, G. (2003, October). The power of audience: Effective communication with your principal. *Library Media Connection,* 22.2, 20.

Hartzell, G. (2003, December). Why should principals support school libraries? *Teacher Librarian,* 31.2, 21-24.

Haycock, K. (1990). Program advocacy: Power, publicity, and the teacher-librarian. *Libraries Unlimited,* n.p.

Haycock, K. (1999). Foundations for effective school library media programs. *Libraries Unlimited,* n.p.

Hylen, J. (2004, May-June). The top ten reasons a library media specialist is a teacher's best friend. *The Clearing House,* 77.5, 219-221.

ILMS Institute of Museum and Library Services, ed. 2002. White House conference examines role of school libraries in education. White House conference on school libraries. Washington, D.C.: IMLS, 2002. 18 June 2005 http://www.imls.gov/pubs/whitehouse0602/whitehouse.htm.

Jimenez, D. (2004, Mar. 25). School librarians expand students' horizons. *Herald–Zeitung,* p. 1A.

Johns, S. K. (2004, September-October). Inspiration. *Knowledge Quest,* 33.1, 18-19.

Johnson, D. (1997). The indispensable librarian: Surviving (and thriving) in school media centers in the information age. Worthington, OH: Linworth.

Johnson, D. (2005, February). Strategies for assisting library media specialists whose positions are in jeopardy. Library Media Connection, 23.5, 44-46. EBSCOEducation. EBSCO. New Braunfels Public Lib. New Braunfels, TX. Retrieved June, 11 2005 from http://search.epnet.com/

Kachel, D. E., Adjunct Instructor. (2005, February 21). LSC 6600 School Library Advocacy for Administrators. Course home page. Summer 2005. Mansfield U. School Lib. & Information Technologies Program. Education Abstracts. EBSCO. New Braunfels Public Lib., New Braunfels, TX. Retrieved May 12, 2005 from http://libweb.mansfield.edu/principals/syllabus.asp

Knezek, J. (2005). What does excellence look like? AASL 2004 National School Library Media Program of the Year Award. Hill Country Librarians Conf. San Antonio, TX: Northside ISD.

Krashen, S. (1993). *The power of reading.* Englewood, CO: Libraries Unlimited.

Lamb, A., & Johnson, L. (2004, December 31). The school library media specialist: School library advocacy program. School of Lib. & Information Science at Purdue U. March-April 2005 http://eduscapes.com/sms/advocacy.html

Lance, K. C. (2002). How school librarians leave no child behind: The impact of school library media programs on academic achievement of U.S. public school students. *School Libraries in Canada,* 22.2, 3-6. Professional Development Collection. EBSCO. New Braunfels Pub. Lib. New Braunfels, TX. Retrieved June 14, 2005 from http://search.epnet.com/login.aspx?direct=true&db=tfh&an=8561105

Lance, K. C. (2004, February-March). Libraries called key. Reading Today, 21.4, 1-2. ERIC. EBSCO. New Braunfels Pub. Lib. New Braunfels, TX. Retrieved June 13, 2005 http://search.epnet.com/login.aspx?direct=true&db=tfh&an=12231611

Mathews, V. (1997, March). Kids can't wait ... library advocacy now! *School Library Journal,* 43.3, 97+.

McNew, C., & Lankford, M. (2001, Summer). Texas school libraries: Standards, resources, services, and students' performance. *Texas Library Journal,* 77.2, 48-52.

Newman, W. and Bauer, V. Incitement to advocate: Advocacy education of future librarians at University of Toronto's Faculty of Information Studies. Feliciter 51.1 (2005): 41-11 Professional Development Collection. EBSCO. New Braunfels Pub. Lib. New Braunfels, TX. 17 Jun. 2005. http://search.epnet.com/login.aspx?direct=true&db=tfh&an=16436929.

Moore, J.A. (2001). The power and promise of partnerships. *Texas Library Journal* 77.1 (Spring 2001): 8-13.

Penny, S. (2004, April 9). Certified librarians play a vital role in educational systems. *Herald–Zeitung,* p. 4A.

Perkins, J. (2005, January). Is anyone out there? *School Library Journal,* 51.1, 13. Professional Development Collection. EBSCO. New Braunfels Pub. Lib. New Braunfels, TX. Retrieve June 14, 2005 from http://search.epnet.com/login.aspx?direct=true&db=tfh&an=15630282

Shuman, P. G. (1999, October). Speaking up and speaking out: Ensuring equity through advocacy. *American Libraries,* 30.9, 50-54.

St. Lifer, E. (2004, October). Getting in the principal's face. *School Library Journal, 50.10, 11.* Professional Development Collection. EBSCO. New Braunfels Pub. Lib. New Braunfels, TX. Retrieved June 14, 2005 from http://search.epnet.com/login.aspx?direct=true&db=tfh&an=14694764

Texas Library Association. (2005). *Join Friends of School Libraries of Texas.* Austin, TX: TLA.

Texas State Libraries & Archives Commission. (2005, May 16). 2005 school library programs: Standards and guidelines for Texas. Texas State Library and Archives. Texas Education Agency. Retrieved June 15, 2005 from http://www.tsl.state.tx.us/ld/schoollibs/

Texas State Libraries & Archives Commission. (2001). Texas school libraries: Standards, resources, services, and students' performance by Ester Smith. Austin, TX: Texas State Lib. and Archives Commission.

Whelan, D. L. (2003, July). Libraries boost student learning. *School Library Journal,* 49.7, 24-25.

Wilson, P. J., & Blake, M. (1993, Spring). The missing piece: A school library media center component in principal-preparation programs. *Educational Administration and Supervision,* 13.2, 65-68.

Additional Resources

American Association of School Librarians. (1999). *A planning guide for information power: Building partnerships for learning with school library media program assessment rubric or the 21st century.* Chicago: ALA.

American Association of School Librarians. (2000). *The principal's manual for your school library media program.* Chicago: ALA.

Colorado State Library, Colorado Department of Education, & Library & Information Science Program at the Univ. of Denver. (2004, June 30). The Colorado advocacy project. *Library Research Service* ED3/110.10.208, 1-2.

Epstein, J. L., & Clark Salinas, K. (2004, May). Partnering with families and communities. *Educational Leadership,* 61.8, 12+.

Fairbanks, M. (2004, June). Building influence for the school librarian: Tenets, targets, & tactics. *School Library Journal,* 50.6, 183+.

Hartzell, G. (2002, September-October). One-sided insight: The 'information center' metaphor. *School Library Journal,* 21.2, 18-19.

Lance, K. C. (1993). *The impact of school library media centers on academic achievement.* Castle Rock, CO: Hi Willow Research and Pub.

Lance, K. C., & Loertscher, D. V. (2003). *Powering achievement: School library media programs make a difference:* The evidence, 2nd ed. Salt Lake City, UT: Hi Willow Research and Pub.

Lawrence, K., & Loertscher, D. (2003). *Powering achievement: School library media programs make a difference—The evidence.* Salt Lake City, UT: Hi Willow Research and Pub.

Loertscher, D. (2002). *Reinventing your school's library in the age of technology: A guide for principals and superintendents.* San Jose, CA: Hi Willow Research and Pub.

Loertscher, D., ed. (2002). *Reinventing your school's library in the age of technology: A guide for principals and superintendents.* Salt Lake City, UT: Hi Willow Research and Pub.

Loertscher, D., & Achterman, D. (2002). *Increasing academic achievement through the library media center: A guide for teachers.* Salt Lake City, UT: Hi Willow Research and Pub.

Loertscher, D. V., & Todd, R. J. (2003). *We boost achievement: Evidence-based practice for school library media specialists.* San Jose, CA: Hi Willow Research.

McGhee, M. W., & Jansen, B.A. (2005). *The principal's guide to a powerful library media program.* Worthington, OH: Linworth Pub.

Young, T. E., Jr. (2004, September-October). Becoming the best at what you do. *Knowledge Quest,* 33.1, 13-14.

CHAPTER FOUR: COLLECTION DEVELOPMENT

Betty Carter

Creating a Collection Development Plan

Collection development is the one professional activity that allows librarians to define the coin of their realms: the content and kinds of materials they can offer the patrons they serve. Collection development begins with a collection development plan that underscores the mission of both the school library and the school system within which it operates, the goals and objectives of the two organizations, and the role of the librarian. The collection development plan defines the patrons, addresses budget allocations, and outlines procedures for selection and de-selection of materials. Good libraries have adequate collection development plans; great libraries have strong ones.

In many ways creating a collection development plan can be compared to establishing a grocery store. Prospective storeowners decide on their mission and their clientele (from pick-up shoppers purchasing gas and convenience items to high-end shoppers looking for exotic spices and the finest cuts of meat to shoppers primarily interested in buying basic food items for family meals) when they establish their businesses. That's why we can find the highest concentration of snack foods at corner convenience stores, sweetbreads at the specialty store, and a large supply of chicken breasts at the family-oriented store. The products, or holdings of each establishment, define both the store's mission (such as convenience or specialty) and the individuals (from commuters to chefs) it is serving. The stores have also made budget decisions: how much space (and consequently the funds to fill that space with merchandise) will be devoted to refrigerated items, to meat products, to personal grooming items, and the like. And stores make decisions about removing items from the shelves, using such guidelines as use-by dates or seasonal demand. Their collection development plan is the blueprint that also guides so many other decisions such as hours of operation, staffing, marketing plans, and service.

Commercial grocery stores enjoy (or tolerate as the case may be) numerous stakeholders such as financial partners, architects, customers, and food and drug policy administrators at all levels. Their development and marketing plans involve each just as a librarian's collection development plan considers a number of individuals and policies: administrators, parents, teachers, students, budgets, the district selection policy, and the like. Without considering these individuals and conditions, librarians will wind up creating fine plans on paper but plans unworkable in the particular schools they were designed for.

As you begin formulating a collection development plan, think of yourself as opening a store. Ask yourself these questions:

What Is My Mission?

First look at the mission statement of the school district. These are not empty words, but are the backbone of your program. Often districts will have terms such as "encourage life long learning" or "realize the educational potential of each student" or "provide students with the tools to become productive citizens" within their mission. Others, particularly private schools, may operate with a mission to establish certain values. Each kind of statement speaks to the kinds and numbers of materials librarians will have in their collections.

For example, educators recognize that youngsters can never realize their educational potential if the only materials available to them are a single textbook in each class. Consequently, materials that directly support classroom teaching in terms of subject (Caroline Arnold's *Pterosaurs: Rulers of the Skies in the Dinosaur Age* details many of the over 100 species of "winged lizards") and process (Dr. Karen Chin and Thom Holmes's *Dino Dung: The Scoop on Fossil Feces* stresses one way in which scientists study animals long since extinct) would both complement a fourth grade curriculum study of dinosaurs. But fourth graders (and all other students) can only realize their educational potential if they also have opportunities to practice the skills developed in the classroom, if they read for pleasure, or engage in mathematical or literary constructs, for example. And although for many *Pterosaurs* and *Dino Dung* may represent pleasure reading, for others books such as Carolyn Coman's *The Big House* (it's highly unlikely that the curriculum directly covers subjects such as freeing a family of charlatans from prison) or Blue Balliett's *Chasing Vermeer* (while pentaminoes are frequently identified, their roles as addictive mathematical puzzles typically receive a short shrift) or Polly Horvath's *The Pepins and Their Problems* (with strong meta-fictive elements typically outside fourth grade language arts inquiry) will bring the joy that encourages youngsters to engage in further reading on their own. These books more than likely lie outside the confines of the curriculum but they have the potential of extending the skills taught therein or of introducing others seldom mentioned. A collection development plan that limits the library's holdings only to subjects directly included in the curriculum will deny youngsters the opportunities to reach their full educational potential.

After studying the district's mission, see if the mission of the particular school you are in adds other information. A science/technology magnet school might exist to prepare students to enter scientific fields, while another campus might have as its mission to prepare youngsters to enter a select group of professions. The mission statements of both an individual school and the district in which it resides should be a part of your collection development plan. In realistic terms, these kinds of statements will allow the librarian to focus on certain materials. Books for preschoolers would at first glance appear to be out of context in a high school library, but if that high school has a mission (and a corresponding curriculum) to prepare students to work as caregivers for the young, then such books are a natural fit within the goals of the school. In this case, a book such as Marc Simot's *The Stray Dog* isn't purchased because the librarian likes dogs, or even because it is a Caldecott medal honor book, but because it allows students opportunities to evaluate materials in their chosen careers and practice that all-important skill of reading aloud.

Who Are My Patrons?

In a school library, the obvious answer is students. But even this answer brings up certain questions. In some settings, all students do not have equal access to the materials. Kindergarten youngsters, for example, sometimes have limited opportunities to circulate library books. In such a case, the question is: Will the library need as many materials in a non-circulating collection as in one that full access is expected? There are other kinds of decisions about patrons.

Some schools, for example, expand the philosophy of promoting learning to the community. In many of those cases, parents freely circulate the library materials. Consequently, the collection development plan should address this population and the kinds of materials that will fall within the school's mission and simultaneously serve them. Does the school fully expect parents to circulate materials kindergarten children are often discouraged from taking home? Are parents who may not have English as their first language encouraged to circulate materials in English that may enhance their own literacy? Or, are parents encouraged to circulate materials on childcare as a way of becoming full partners in the educational system? Reread the mission of your district and of your school to decide which services fall within the goals of the institution. If so, acquisition and circulation of such materials must be explicitly stated in the collection development plan. Otherwise, they become noble ideas that exist as tangential pieces to the educational program. Not only will they become underused mini-collections, but they will also be the first eliminated in budget cuts.

Consider teachers. Are materials in the library collected for teachers' professional growth, or is there another site within the district that fulfills this charge? Some librarians collect popular reading material for teachers. The philosophy behind this decision comes straight from the district's mission to encourage reading among the children served. In these cases, librarians have reasoned that it takes readers to encourage readers, and that by offering popular titles in the library they can (1) ensure some teacher traffic and create opportunities to talk about reading and perhaps extend those talks to children's materials and (2) create a community of readers that may by association foster an environment that encourages everyone to read. With these objectives outlined in a collection development plan, librarians can protect these holdings and contribute to the goals of the school.

What Kinds of Materials Will Be Included in the Collection?

School libraries cannot exist with collections comprised completely of books, nor can they rely on electronic services for all their needs. Conscious decisions must be made about the kind of materials—electronic databases, books (specifying both formats and language), newspapers, magazines, books on tape, DVDs, picture files— that will be included in the collection and which ones will not. Those that will be included should be actively collected, however. For example, if pamphlets are accepted, then that acceptance shouldn't just depend on allowing the stray one to enter into the collection. Decisions about housing and cataloging should be made before hand; the librarian should have in mind the kinds of pamphlets needed and obtain them. If certain kinds of materials (pamphlets in this example) aren't a visible, active part of the collection, then they are often overlooked in inquiry and discounted as "real" sources or "real" library materials.

Sometimes those considerations may deal with virtual formats. Vertical files, for example, were once a staple in school libraries. Such files, typically organized in a number of cabinets with subject headings, contained clippings, community resources, pamphlets, product descriptions, and other kinds of ephemera related to a particular subject.

In today's world, computer folders with appropriate bookmarks frequently replace the row of file cabinets that once stored these paper treasures. Now, as professional compilations of a well-trained librarian, these electronic folders represent a part of the collection. Not only should they be catalogued so youngsters can access them on their own, as they once plundered through drawers of the vertical file, but they should also be noted in a collection development plan. Their inclusion, and their use, give a frame of reference for observers who see librarians spending great amounts of time on the Internet and underscore the advanced searching skills librarians bring to their jobs.

How Will the Materials Be Selected?

Before addressing this portion of the campus collection development plan, revisit the district's selection policy. (If there is no district-wide selection policy there is no professional climate within which to run a library. The situation could be compared to running a school district without a curriculum.) These guidelines are the ones to follow. Perhaps there are problems with the selection policy, such as an ironclad rule that materials must have two positive journal reviews for inclusion. Since such absolutes can, for example, eliminate many locally produced materials and books, librarians may want to amend the statement by letting the professional opinions of two district librarians substitute for a pair of published reviews. Still, these new practices can't begin until the school board approves the amended policy.

Even with clear-cut district guidelines, librarians balance a number of considerations as they select books. They consider content, curricula connections, reading interests and the like. Selecting materials is both an art and a science. Libraries are defined by their collections; librarians are defined by their attention to these holdings.

In 1999 school librarian Janice Freiheit investigated the selection practices of librarians in one Texas school district. She asked the librarians how they should be selecting materials. Overwhelmingly, they outlined many of the steps discussed below. She then asked them if they were able to follow these principles. Overwhelmingly, they confessed that "no they weren't." The reason? They were spending so much of their time creating lessons for teachers. She further asked how they were selecting books, and again a large number of librarians responded in kind: They were getting their suggestions from teachers, from lists of books mentioned in professional growth workshops, from subject oriented catalogs, and from word of mouth. There is a lot wrong with this picture.

Librarians have advanced training in selection; they are the one professional group that has adopted policies that ensure focused but well-rounded collections. Yes, they have an instructional role in the school, but that role should never obliterate the skills and responsibilities they bring to their jobs as librarians. And teachers have specialized knowledge about their subjects that can serve librarians well in selecting materials, but that knowledge should never obliterate the planning and teaching skills and responsibilities they bring to their jobs as classroom teachers. Each should act as advisor and consultant to the other's strengths rather than as an usurper of other's responsibilities. Thus, the question remains: What should librarians bring to the process of selecting materials?

Retrospective Selection

Begin at the beginning. Librarians should have a strong idea of what kinds of materials they are looking for. A number of publishers and jobbers have taken various state curricula, matched them to their offerings, and provided librarians with a matrix of books and media that match these subjects and objectives. So, why not simply order the materials that intersect with the curriculum topics on your campus? Two reasons: (1) the books might have internal problems such as similarity in presentation, incorrect content, or insipid writing and (2) all subjects and objectives in a curriculum outline do not necessarily receive the same treatment in every classroom or on every campus.

David Loertscher's *Taxonomies of the School Library Media Program* details a plan for curriculum mapping so librarians can ascertain precisely what is being taught on their respective campuses and in what areas teachers wish to make the most use of library resources. Following Loertscher's curriculum mapping, librarians can evaluate sections of the existing collection, order materials to fill in deficiencies, and create a practical collection development strategy, all the while using teacher input that relates directly to class instruction. A word of caution: the task of curriculum mapping is daunting, and one that cannot be completed in a single year. Select carefully the areas you wish to examine, prioritize them, and begin a systematic process of matching resources to the content of the classrooms. But remember, curriculum mapping is not a finite process; teachers alter plans every year, districts adopt new textbooks, and states require new benchmarks for student learning.

It is also important to remember that curriculum mapping alone cannot give the necessary information for a complete collection development plan. Librarians might attempt a focused analysis of the collection by, for example, selecting every fifth book and categorizing that book by descriptors, such as most targeted grade level, a leisure reading/curriculum designation (which may sometimes overlap), genre, or a represented subject. By compiling these rough statistics, librarians will discover other areas to target for collection development.

Through curriculum mapping, a librarian might discover that a fourth grade content study on arachnids will result in a teacher assigning youngsters to select an arachnid and be prepared to identify the features that define it as a member of that class of animals. The librarian will need materials with illustrations, such as photographs, drawings, or diagrams, to make this classroom assignment succeed. According to the teacher in question, youngsters will work in pairs, and classes typically contain about 22 students with varying degrees of reading sophistication. This small project should not necessitate overnight checkouts, so the librarian can estimate that he or she will need about 15 separate sources. Assuming that there are five computers in the library with Internet connections or access to an encyclopedia such as *World Book* (which at this writing contained only a single diagram of one arachnid, a spider), then at least 10 additional print sources must be found. A quick check of the present collection shows only five such books, so the librarian will need to order at least five additional ones.

Here is where both the art and the science of book selection come into play. Going back to the grocery story analogy for a moment put yourself in the role of the consumer. Assume you are trying to eat healthy. You could outline the food pyramid and ask the grocer to send you enough meat, dairy products, and vegetables to satisfy those standards for meals for a family of four for a week. Clearly shoppers disdain such shopping methods, which may result in healthy foods but some strange menu combinations. Even with online shopping services, they want to select the items that will meet their family's needs, budgets, and tastes. Librarians must do the same.

To visit a jobber's Web site and select all offerings on spiders would be akin to the example above of simply requesting food. The science of selection (searching for materials that fit into curricula subjects) is certainly present, but not the art (identifying and ordering materials at different levels, that contain different examples, and that include different approaches to the subject). A recent examination of Title Wave (http://www.follett.com) under the subject of "Spiders," turned up some fine books such as Seymour Simon's *Spiders* and Marjorie Facklam's *Spiders and Their Web Sites*, each with great potential for the assignment. What didn't show up were three additional titles that appear to have great relevance to this particular project—Melvin Berger's *Spinning Spiders*, an entry in the Let's Read and Find Out About Science series; Sharon Gordon's *Guess Who Spins* from the Guess Who series; or John Towsend's *Incredible Arachnids* from the Incredible Creatures series—even though separate title searches revealed that Follett was able to provide those particular books. Products such as Title Wave can prove tremendously helpful as sources for reviews and as ancillary collection analysis tools, but as the sole providers of retrospective selection, they have their weaknesses.

So, where do other titles come from? The Berger book, *Spinning Spiders*, emerged from *Children's Catalog*, a long-standard retrospective selection aid from H. W. Wilson. *Children's Catalog*, and the corresponding catalogs for schools serving older children, *Middle and Junior High School Catalog* and *Senior High School Catalog*, identifies what a team of respected librarians and critics has defined as a core collection. Each respective team has collectively studied both general curriculum topics and leisure reading selections by examining the available books in each area. Every school in a particular district may not need to house a copy of the appropriate catalog, but the catalogs should be available, either in print or online form, to the collective body of district librarians, particularly for use in identifying core books for new areas of inquiry. Not all mentioned books will necessarily complement assignments, although they are typically considered worthy of library purchase. For example, Darlyne Murawski's *Spiders and Their Webs*, which did not show up in the Title Wave search, apparently concentrates on making and using webs, a related topic to the curriculum but one that may not satisfy the particular assignment under investigation.

The other two books mentioned above, *Guess Who Spins* and *Incredible Arachnids*, came from the Spring 2005 issue of *The Horn Book Guide*. *The Horn Book Guide* provides short annotations of the majority of hardcover trade books published in the United States during the previous six-month period. In addition to these annotations, reviewers assign numerical ratings with one indicating that the book is outstanding and six indicting that the book is unacceptable. The subject index allows librarians to search by topic and provides a quick resource for updating areas of need. The books *Guess Who Spins* and *Incredible Arachnids* were neither originally reviewed in *The Horn Book Magazine* but both received a Guide rating of 3, indicating that they were recommended for purchase although not necessarily a first purchase.

Still, librarians must move beyond a single source for recommendations. A quick check of Amazon.com revealed that neither book had been reviewed in the posted sources, but a check of Title Wave cited additional review sources for librarians to consult. In other words, it takes a village of sources to find, identify, and create a strong collection.

Librarians will, of course, move beyond trade books as they seek other sources. They could bookmark Web sites such as *Everything About Arachnids* (http://www.everythingabout.net/articles/biology/animals/arthropods/arachnids/), which has photographs and information for some under-addressed animals such as ticks.

In keeping with the old saying, "A librarian's work is never done," the process is far from over. First, keep track of the procedure. This record is but one concrete way in which librarians can begin to quantify the kind of work they do, work that is often overlooked and undervalued. Second, compute the amount of money spent in satisfying this one area of support. With the average price of a children's/young adult book being $20.52 (St. Lifer, 2005), the cost for ordering the aforementioned five books is approximately $146. These kinds of figures can impact future budget decisions (see #5). Third, ask other librarians in the district if they could profit from your search; if they can, then share the process with them. And fourth, now look over the collection. It might be heavy in books that satisfy this assignment, but low on tangential areas such as spinning webs featured in Murawski's *Spiders and Their Webs* or in the work of scientists in the field, covered beautifully in Sy Montgomery's *The Tarantula Scientist*. Perhaps books that approach the topic of arachnids indirectly, such as Doreen Cronin's Diary of a Spider or Jean Craighead George's *The Tarantula in My Purse* and *172 Other Wild Pets*, could also extend this curricula subject. Are these kinds of books also available? If not, then further collection development is in order.

This last activity assumes one critical piece of collection development: the librarian knows the collection. That knowledge can only come through wide reading. The payoff, however, is incalculable. Librarians who are readers, who read beyond their own interests and personal tastes, create students who are also readers. So with a single activity, that of reading the books in the collection, librarians can begin to ensure that the materials they house will not only be selected wisely but ultimately used.

Ongoing Selection

Retrospective collection development is only one part of a librarian's accountability. There's also a responsibility to keep the present collection up to date, to anticipate needs, and respond to the reading interests of the population served. The process refers to the purchase of new materials, as well as the treatment of gift items. It is a job no one person can fulfill without help, and in this case, the librarian's best help comes through using a combination of review journals.

In times of budget crisis, librarians may be tempted to cut their review journal subscriptions under the misinformed notion that their budget money will all be going directly to the youngsters they serve. This kind of thinking doesn't serve either the librarian or the patrons well. When money is short, the reverse is true: librarians need every ounce of help possible to make the most informed decisions about the small number of materials they will purchase.

Full text reviews of books are available in many places beyond the pages of established review journals, although often key elements from the print versions are missing from electronic ones (the repeat notes in *Booklist* (see page 65) do not show up on commercial databases such as Amazon.com and *The Horn Book Guide* reviews are frequently indistinguishable from *The Horn Book Magazine* reviews (see page 65-66) and the crucial *Guide* numerical ratings are eliminated from databases such as Title Wave). Web booksellers, in the business of selling books, frequently choose not to print negative reviews even though they print positive reviews from a particular journal.

But of greater importance is that librarians who first operate from a list of titles not generated by review journals are consistently building a collection that is reactive rather than proactive. At the end of the day, someone else is suggesting the universe of books from which the librarian will choose. Review journals, some of which address everything that is published, others that narrow the pool in a variety of ways, nonetheless operate within a system that is defensible and understandable, and ultimately more reliable than lists generated by individuals, commercial entities, and organizations with their own agendas.

Furthermore, even review journals that publish only reviews (such as *The Bulletin*) initiate a conversation about books and media that librarians must be involved in. Review journals take librarians away from the confines of their individual campuses by offering differing opinions and jumpstarting internal musings about the literary world in general or about particular books and media. That dialogue between writer and reader may come through articles or recommendations for readers' advisory or new items, or it may come by giving the librarian an opportunity to see what's available, from "hot" books to trends in publishing. The available books and materials can alert librarians to upcoming events (such as the anniversary of the Wright Brothers flight, Dr. Seuss' birthday, constitution day, or the 100 year marker for Einstein's theories) that will require additional materials. These are the kinds of conversations that allow professionals to consider the heart of the program they are administering.

Sometimes a review will call attention to a book critical in the present curriculum, sometimes a review will cover a book that a librarian might not have considered ordering, and sometimes a review will suggest alternative ways of looking at media. Roger Sutton, executive editor of *Horn Book*, remarked that all the pieces of the magazine and the guide were both available somewhere on the Internet. The problem was that librarians had to know what they were looking for in order to find them; a page-by-page reproduction of the print journals is not available (Sutton, 2005). Consequently, while a librarian may be able to locate a particular article, related topics covered in the same journal might well escape notice and thus be lost to the professional's attention. It also follows that librarians are unable to locate a journal's review only if they have a particular book in mind to begin with.

Careful use of review journals also allows librarians to make informed decisions about the materials they select. Not only do they widen the pool of materials from which to choose, but they also mitigate the chance of having collections reflecting the personal taste of the librarian in charge. As a fan of realistic fiction over fantasy, I would tend to neglect the latter without the push to remember what review journals provide.

Librarians who use review journals also protect themselves and their professional decisions. District selection policies, often reproduced from the model provided by the National Association of School Boards, typically require two positive reviews for materials selected for collections. This kind of provision allows for differing opinions, and, when adopted, effectively supports librarians who order materials that meet these requirements. In intellectual freedom challenges, that support, even though it may appear to be tacit, helps keep responses professional rather than personal. Librarians who order materials solely because they like them or because someone recommended them are subject to values debates (my ideas are better than yours) in times of intellectual freedom discussions. Librarians who adhere to strong selection policies can offer a professional detour from that path.

No single review journal, no matter how respected, will adequately serve a school librarian. Reviews are by nature subjective, and individuals, no matter what their level of experience and expertise, approach books in different ways. Because of the subjective nature of reviews, it's not only possible, but also highly likely that a book will receive a glowing review in one journal and a negative review in another. For that reason, the conventional wisdom follows that subscriptions to at least three journals are a necessity.

There are five journals that primarily address the needs of children's and young adult selectors in K-12 schools. Two others deal with children's materials but in different contexts. *Kirkus Reviews* primarily addresses public librarians and *Publishers Weekly* has as its main audience booksellers. In addition, secondary school librarians will profit from subscriptions to journals such as *Library Journal* that reviews adult books (of particular interest to high school librarians) or specialty journals such as *Science Books & Films*. These journals are both informative and helpful, but the five that appear on pages 65-66 best meet the general needs of school librarians. The thumbnail sketches of each provide but mere starting places for making decisions about which journals best suit individual needs. Further information is available on indicated Web sites.

Booklist <http://www.ala.org/ala/booklist/booklist.htm> is the official book review journal of the American Library Association. Books reviewed in *Booklist* are recommended for purchase in school libraries and small- and medium-sized public libraries. Therefore, a book that doesn't have a *Booklist* review, has, in effect, received a negative review. It is not recommended for purchase. When someone questions a book that doesn't receive a *Booklist* review it's natural to think that perhaps the editors didn't see it. They saw it; they get multiple copies of everything published and will either review or reject materials within three months of publication. Media, reference materials, and online subscription services are also reviewed. In addition, because *Booklist* serves both public and school libraries, it covers adult books and targets those adult books of interest to high school librarians with repeat notes signifying the areas of strength.

The staff at *Booklist* includes a cadre of professional reviewers, who are salaried with full-time jobs to review and edit new publications from publishers. Their advantage is that they examine hundreds, even thousands, of books every year and know the field. *Booklist* also employs outside reviewers who work on consignment. Their advantage is that they bring fresh/different voices to the review process, and, if they can work closely with someone seeing tons of books, the two together can make a strong contribution. *Booklist* denotes books of distinction by a star, starring approximately five to 10 juvenile books per bi-monthly issue.

The Bulletin for the Center of Children's Books, or *The Bulletin* <http://bccb.lis.uiuc.edu/>, operates out of the University of Illinois and reviews books published expressly for children and young adults. *The Bulletin* is selective about the books it reviews, choosing books that the editorial staff thinks contain something subscribers want to know about, whether it be subject or theme or approach or characterization or curriculum use. With the longest reviews of any of the journals, *The Bulletin's* reviewers have the space to say what they think is important and to discuss many facets of the books under review. *The Bulletin* reviews about 80-90 books each month; the journal comes out 11 times a year.

The Bulletin uses a rating system: a star for a book outstanding in its genre; an R, which means recommended for purchase, and an AD, which indicates a book of acceptable quality and fine for libraries needing more material or stories like the one reviewed. An M indicates a marginal purchase, while an NR means Not Recommended and a SR indicates Special Reader. *The Bulletin* stars about two books each issue.

The Bulletin uses a small review staff, some full time, some part time. These reviewers live in the same geographical area and meet to make decisions about books, or discuss individual reviews on a regular basis. There is more lag time between date of publication and reviews for *The Bulletin* than any other journal; reviews of books from a current calendar year may appear three months into the next year. This flexibility with dates, however, allows *The Bulletin* to publish many reviews from small press publishers who do not routinely distribute advanced reading copies of books.

The Horn Book Magazine and *The Horn Book Guide* <http://www.hbook.com/> are complementary journals. As in *Booklist,* reviews in *The Horn Book Magazine* indicate a recommendation for purchase. Unlike *Booklist,* though, books not reviewed in *The Horn Book Magazine* are not necessarily books the staff wouldn't recommend for purchase for a library. They are frequently books that are judged to be "just OK, nothing special," much like the AD recommendation in *The Bulletin*. And, like *The Bulletin*, both *The Horn Book Magazine* and *The Horn Book Guide* only review books published expressly for children and young adults, although audio books are also reviewed in the magazine. One other similarity must be noted; in recent years both *The Horn Book Magazine* and *The Bulletin* have increased their coverage of young adult offerings. At one time both journals had the reputation of primarily addressing books for young children; that reputation is no longer justified.

The Horn Book Magazine's reviewing staff is small, centered on a professional cadre in Boston. Other reviewers are scattered around the country, each chosen because of a particular strength or area of expertise. Although the reviewers don't meet often, they do have an active closed discussion list that allows one person to ask others to look at a particular book or to study a particular feature. Reviewers for *The Horn Book Guide* are more numerous and more diverse. Each is identified with professional affiliations in a separate appendix in each issue.

In selecting which books to send for review in *The Horn Book Magazine,* and which books to send for review in *The Horn Book Guide,* the editors keep in mind the original mission of the magazine: to review the best of children's literature. Within that charge, they attempt to balance genres among picture books, chapter fiction, nonfiction, poetry, and folklore and will often select books with underserved topics. But they also have a back-up system with the reviewers. *Guide* reviewers will frequently alert the magazine's staff that a particular book should be addressed in that publication while magazine reviewers will frequently submit some of their reviews exclusively for the *Guide*. Books are reviewed in the calendar year in which they are published, with the one exception being the January issue of the next year that will include publications from the previous year. *The Horn Book Magazine* is published every other month and reviews about 80 books every issue, with an average of five stars (denoting exceptional merit) per issue. *The Horn Book Guide* comes out twice a year.

The Horn Book Guide prints short, critical summaries (about 60 words per book) of the reviewed books and covers the majority of publications from juvenile publishers. Each book receives a numerical rating: 1 is outstanding; 2 is superior; 3 is recommended or satisfactory; 4 is recommended with minor flaws; 5 is marginal; and 6 is unacceptable.

School Library Journal (SLJ) <http://www.schoollibraryjournal.com/> reviews media (including subscription databases, DVDs, audio books) and books (including some adult books and reference materials) for children in grades K-12. Librarians in the field review the majority of books for *School Library Journal.* These active professionals bring a practical view to the reviews, noting where, in their experience, materials are useful for group activities or curriculum tie-ins. These reviewers typically receive two-four books each month. *SLJ* reviews the majority of children's and young adult trade publications, so the journal contains both positive and negative reviews. This journal sees its mission as one of providing a buying guide for librarians. Reviews generally appear within three months of a book's original publication date. *SLJ* stars about 20 books in each monthly issue.

VOYA: Voice of Youth Advocates in Libraries (http://www.voya.com) exclusively addresses librarians and educators who serve young adults. This bimonthly publication reviews books (including adult publications and reference books) and non-print (including electronic media, audio books, and DVDs) materials for youngsters in grades 6-12. *VOYA* gives special attention to books in different formats such as graphic novels, series (both fiction and nonfiction) books, and e-books. Reviewers work directly with young adults. Each reviewer receives books/media that correspond with his or her special interests and expertise.

As a journal that has as part of its mission to serve as an advocate for teens, *VOYA* employs a unique rating scale for books, summing up each review in terms of popularity and quality. Each feature receives a numerical rating from 1-5, with a 5P indicating that readers are clamoring for it and a 1P indicating that teens will only read this one if forced. In terms of quality, a 5Q indicates masterful writing, while a 1Q questions how the book ever got published in the first place. Books can receive 5P and 1Q or a 1P and a 5Q or any combination in between. In selecting which combination of journals best meets their needs, librarians will consider and balance many elements such as numbers and focus of reviews, full-time vs. part-time reviewers, and other features of the journals that are important in professional growth. And remember, if budgets are tight, it's possible to stretch those review dollars by partnering with a neighboring campus and making it possible for two librarians to order and share unique journals. Information is power, and the more information librarians have about the materials they're ordering, the higher the potential for a strong, well-defined collection.

Selection must be ongoing. With the myriad complicated responsibilities librarians have, it's easy to put off selection until right before final purchase orders are due in the business office. But such a practice favors impulse shopping over contemplative decisions and doesn't pay off.

Every month read through the new journals, think of what you need, what you want, and what you found that you didn't know you needed or wanted until you saw it. Make a consideration file, marking the most honest reason (such as specific curriculum tie-ins, pleasure reading, underserved topics or subjects, patron interest) for ordering each book. Prioritize the items and then re-examine them. Are there an undue number of books for the Eighth grade science curriculum or an overabundance of historical fiction? Are you heavy in rip-roaring read alouds, but light in quiet books that may appeal to special readers? These questions, that librarians ask (and answer) all during the year, balance the collection in a way that is impossible to create at the last minute.

Occasionally lists from various organizations can help librarians with suggestions of titles that may fill some holes in the collection. For example, if a librarian believes that the collection holds little appeal for children, perhaps a check of Children's Choices, an annual list that represents children's favorites from among a representative sample of the previous year's new publications, could yield additional suggestions. Each book on such lists, however, should be scrutinized through precisely the same lens as all other purchases. The most up-to-date compilation of such lists appears on the Web site of the Cooperative Children's Book Center out of the University of Wisconsin at Madison <http://www.soemadison.wisc.edu/ccbc/books/default.asp>.

Review journals do not tell librarians what to order. They allow librarians to know what's new; what's available; and what someone, who has examined the item carefully and thoughtfully, thinks about it. Don't consider a starred review (or its *VOYA* equivalent of 5P/5Q) a directive for purchase. Yes, the book could well be outstanding, but perhaps it is too young for your patrons, such as a book indicated for preschool youngsters and your campus doesn't house a kindergarten but instead serves grades 1-5. Conversely, don't consider a lukewarm review a necessary rejection. Perhaps the book covers a topic or subject that is underserved in your library and you're willing to trade a less stellar product for basic coverage. A series of books about world cultures might receive a strong review, but if the library already owns the electronic resource, *World Cultures Today,* perhaps that subscription negates the need for a hardcover series. And the decisions go on and on. Perhaps next month the print series on world cultures receives an even stronger review in another journal. In that case, the librarian might rethink the original priority rating.

Selection is far from a solitary pursuit. Route review journals to faculty members and ask for their comments on particular items. Solicit suggestions such as book lists, but treat each such suggestion just as you treat every item under consideration: look up the reviews and weigh each item's place in the collection against its critical reception and the existing resources.

And always remember that the library supports the curriculum; it isn't the curriculum. Many schools, for example, employ electronic reading management programs, such as Accelerated Reader or Reading Counts, as a part (or all) of the reading/English curriculum. And in many such sites, teachers and administrators expect the librarian to order carte blanche lists of books supported by such programs, supplying librarians with the rationale that, "this is part of the curriculum." Particular classrooms and curricular materials can be excluded from the collection development plan. Libraries support the curriculum; they typically do not purchase or house the daily teaching materials such as textbooks (which in many cases these trade books have become). There could, understandably, be some overlap where an entire class might read Gary Paulsen's *Hatchet* and the library owns a couple of copies because of student demand. But the school library should not become the school's textbook warehouse. Vent individual curriculum items through the normal review process and order only those that fit within the library's plan. Otherwise, the focus of the collection will be lost, the place of the library within the school obscured, and the professional strengths of the librarian obliterated.

Librarians who purchase large numbers of trade books solely to support reading management programs or to mirror reading instruction (with books that favor controlled vocabulary and reading skill development over story and student interest) are in grave danger of jeopardizing their mission of promoting lifetime readers. Approximately 15 years ago, the authors of *Becoming a Nation of Readers* reported the problem: "Reading instruction can be boring. Aspects of the standard reading lesson are monotonous. Many of the tasks assigned to children in the name of reading are drudgery. Thus, it is not surprising that . . . interviews with a sample of poor, black children reading a year above grade level indicated that most liked to read, but few liked the activities called 'reading' in school" (Anderson et al., 1985, p. 15).

Just because children are reading trade books assigned by teachers and curriculum mandates does not necessarily mean that they are sentient lifetime readers. In a word, what all too often is missing is choice. A 1996 study from the National Reading Research Center reports that of a group of third and fifth graders asked about the most interesting story read in the past week, only 10 percent cited one assigned by the teacher. Eighty-eight percent of these youngsters chose their favorite stories themselves. Their memorable selections came not from class assignments, but from their own personal interests, often fueled by recommendations from others, familiarity with particular authors and genres, and a fondness for series books (Gambrell et al., 1996).

Children who grow up to become lifetime readers have access to books and make their own choices about what they read. Along with hearing books read aloud on a regular basis and combining reading with social interaction, youngsters must experience these two critical behaviors in order to become lifetime readers. They may be the most in jeopardy.

These are the books that allow youngsters to think about and read about the things they want to think about and read about. These are also the books that entitle them to discover issues and topics that they may have never imagined before they picked up a particular volume. And, these are the books that provide children diversion and escape, frequently by letting them return to familiar authors, genres, series, and topics. Such materials give children meaningful practice with those hard-earned classroom skills. They turn novice readers into professional ones, selecting what they want to read, engaging in the act independently, and deciding both the sequence and the amount of a book or story or article they read.

Many children only discover such books and magazines, and the luxury to select them freely, in their school libraries. Professional librarians understand techniques for working with individual readers who want help and for backing off from those who want to be left alone. Librarians learn not to pass value judgments on what children choose to read. They also learn aggressive measures for protecting well-chosen materials some may want to remove or restrict. In other words, librarians energetically support a student's right to choose and read precisely those materials that encourage lifetime learning. Library leaders begin promoting and protecting these behaviors with their collection development plans.

Intellectual Freedom

Part of any collection development plan must address issues of intellectual freedom. The majority of school librarians chose this profession and the profession is quite clear about the responsibilities to the patrons and to the students' rights to read (related documents can be found on the American Library Association's Web site: http://www.ala.org). The profession has taken a strong stand in opposition to censorship. Apparently, however, some members of the profession do not agree. A recent survey of Texas librarians showed that a full 73 percent of responding school librarians believed that they should exercise censorship in the selection of materials (Hoffman, 2005).

Let's put this debate in its most basic form. Censorship does not mean that librarians suggest placing the most recent Bret Easton Ellis book in elementary libraries. The book is clearly geared toward an adult audience and no review source has suggested otherwise. Censorship, however, does mean that librarians employ unwritten standards for selecting materials. Librarians who believe they should not purchase recommended books that contain particular words they do not wish used (or even words that the school boards have prohibited from campus speech) or address situations they don't like to think about or contain information about practices, such as premarital sex, they would prefer teenagers not engage in, are censors, unless the above mentioned examples are expressly prohibited by the district's board-approved selection policy.

There are many easy excuses, but none masks the ugly truth: Many school librarians are censors. Let's examine a couple of examples. In 1996 Deborah Lockhart studied the holdings of elementary schools within an urban Texas school district. She systematically searched each OPAC, looking to see if librarians purchased books that received starred reviews in two basic review journals. She found that librarians overwhelmingly purchased such books, unless the review indicated that the book dealt with topics of sex or if the reviews mentioned the presence of particular words.

In 2003 I examined the holdings of the majority of Texas public schools looking for books concerning sexuality, including topics of homosexuality, transgendered youth, and safe sex. I found that such topics, if addressed at all, were contained in a handful of fiction books, but were all but absent in the nonfiction collection. If there were exceptions, more likely than not the books appeared in schools that served students older than the intended reader. For example, Robie Harris' *It's So Amazing* was held by twice as many high schools as elementary schools (including those schools that had cataloged the book in a "professional" collection) that represented the target audience. In a series of follow-up interviews, librarians admitted that nonfiction accounts, particularly dealing with safe sex, were the kinds of books they didn't include in their collections, despite the fact that district selection policies did not exclude these topics, because they wanted to avoid any challenges. Such a self-serving excuse may avoid real or imagined conflict, but fails to serve the number of teens who might well contract HIV because they lack the information to prevent it.

In 2004, when Keven Henkes' *Olive's Ocean* was cited as a Newbery Honor book, the announcement created a furor among many librarians posting on electronic discussion lists. How could a book that mentioned that parents engaged in sex be included in an elementary library? What would the parents say? The incident under discussion involves a couple of sentences within a complete novel, but sentences that reinforce the overall theme that deals with the various ways in which family members express love towards one another. Besides receiving a Newbery Honor citation, the book was starred in *Booklist, The Horn Book Magazine,* and *School Library Journal,* and generally recommended as reading for grade five and up. Yet, school librarians supposedly serving fifth and sixth grade youngsters refused to order this book. Since most district policies would allow books with this kind of critical reception in their libraries, clearly the decision not to select *Olive's Ocean* came from some non-publicized scale that librarians applied at will. How sad that many youngsters, who have never seen love expressed between parents, or who have horrible experiences with sex being fueled by alcohol or violence or drugs, are denied this examination of family life because they drew a censorious librarian rather than a professional campus leader.

My daddy was a great bridge player. He often said, "If you make all the slams you bid, you aren't bidding aggressively enough." The same reasoning might apply to library collections: If no one ever complains (either formally or informally), perhaps you have insipid offerings. If schools are to educate children, rather than indoctrinate them, then the library collections should offer a variety of situations, subjects, and themes youngsters may not encounter in their daily lives. A library collection does not reflect the personal beliefs of the librarian. After all, what librarian really believes that animals talk with humans? Books like *Charlotte's Web* clearly recreate that situation, so the practice for collections to contain books that go against some personal beliefs is an accepted one. All materials must be subject to the same standards for inclusion or non-inclusion.

As part of the collection development plan, prepare for challenges by making, or reviewing, a reconsideration plan for challenged materials. (Again, check the ALA Web site for a sample.) Be prepared before a complaint occurs by alerting the school administrator to items that might be challenged and the reasons for inclusion, select the reconsideration team before the challenge occurs, and adhere to the policies of the district. Sure, such practices protect the librarian, but they also protect the students and their right to read books that may enrich their worlds.

Deselecting Materials

A collection development plan should also cover removing books and media from the library, dropping online services, or discontinuing serial subscriptions. The latter two are typically taken care of when librarians assess their purchases and determine if materials are covered in the collection development plan. But the former, or weeding, often receives a short shrift.

Return to the analogy of a grocery store. Think of the stores you may have visited where there's a hodge podge of offerings, the shelves crowded, and cans with tired old labels that just appear old and unappealing. You might pick up a roll of paper towels there, but would often visit another site for food items. As new books come in, as curricula change, as shelves get stuffed, as books get used over and over, school libraries can quickly resemble that dusty old grocery store and hold little appeal for students.

Occasionally librarians will meet resistance to weeding, particularly from those who want to create an illusion of a well-stocked library. Most often that resistance comes within systems that require a set number of books per student with the rationale that the school can't afford to "go below standards." Such standards assume that the prescribed number of books are current and contain potentially meaningful content. The practice of keeping outdated and worn materials creates a false illusion about the library. Neither children nor their teachers have any respect for such a collection and by association both the librarian and the library become ineffective instructional partners.

Weeding the collection is an ongoing process that not only keeps the library vibrant, but that also allows the librarian to advertise its present purpose. Although there are many guidelines available, one of the most comprehensive, *The CREW Manual*, is available in full text format online from The Texas State Library and Archives Division at <http://www.tsl.state.tx.us/ld/pubs/crew/toc.html>.

How Will the Budget Be Allocated?

At one time, budgets for school libraries were created at the top level of the administrative hierarchy and passed down to individual librarians. Administrators allotted a set amount of money and school librarians spent it. But with the advent of site-based management, and library standards stating that libraries should contain the materials necessary for supporting the curriculum and the mission of the school (rather than a set number of books per pupil), librarians finally have the latitude to create their own budgets. In such cases, a strong collection development plan is the librarian's best friend.

Librarians who walk into an administrator's office at budget time with a detailed collection development plan showing the curriculum requirements of different teachers (discovered through curriculum mapping), the replacement costs for lost and damaged materials, and the areas where the collection needs to grow (determined through collection analysis), and match each of these areas with appropriate costs for books, serials, and media, will have a better chance of realizing their needs than will a librarian who just says "I don't have enough money." Ancillary needs (for example, tape recorders to circulate with the audio book collection important to the English department or computers to accommodate students completing specified assignments) addressed in this manner also underscore the role of the library in the overall educational focus of the school. Perhaps that money is not available immediately, but administrators who see a well thought-out plan for spending funds (and who have been reminded of specific needs), can often find additional monies throughout the year. Prepared librarians are ready for such windfalls and since their planned expenditures represent a critical need, can repay an administrator's decision with a strong and visible educational output.

Far from secret documents, collection development plans underscore the goals of the library program, the mission of the library, and the work of the librarian. They are both deliberative and informative, and reinforce the professional role of the school librarian. They are created and defended by leaders who aim for the highest level of service. Librarians can plead "no time" and ignore collection development. Or, they can approach the task professionally and carefully and in so doing create great library programs.

Works Cited

American Library Association. Last accessed August 2005 at http://www.ala.org

Anderson, R.C., Hiebert, E. H., Scott, J. A., & Wilkinson, I. A. G. (1985). *Becoming a nation of readers: The report of the commission on reading.* Washington, DC: National Institute of Education.

Arnold, C. (2004). *Pterosaurs: Rulers of the skies in the dinosaur age.* New York: Clarion.

Balliett, B. (2005). *Chasing Vermeer.* New York: Scholastic.

Berger, M. (2003). *Spinning spiders.* New York: HarperCollins.

Carter, B. (2003). Booktalking Gay and Lesbian Literature. Paper presented at the Texas Library Association's Annual Conference, Houston, TX.

Children's Catalog. Accessed through Wilson Web, August 2005 at http://www.wilsonweb.com

Chin, K., & Holmes, T. (2005). *Dino dung: The scoop on fossil feces.* New York: Random.

Coman, C. (2004). *The big house.* Ashville, NC: Front Street.

Cooperative Children's Book Center. Last accessed August 2005 at http://www.soemadison.wisc.edu/ccbc/books/default.asp

The CREW Manual. Last accessed August 2005 at http://www.tsl.state.tx.us/ld/pubs/crew/toc.html

Cronin, D. (2005). *Diary of a spider.* New York: Joanna Colter Books/HarperCollins.

Freiheit, J. (1999). The Use of Professional Selection Tools by School Library Media Specialists in the Dallas Public Schools, Master's Paper, Texas Woman's University: Denton, TX.

Gambrell, L. B. et al. (1996). *Elementary students' motivation to read: Reading research report no. 52.* Washington: Office of Educational Research and Improvement. ERIC Document 395 279.

George, J. (1996). *The tarantula in my purse and 172 other wild pets.* New York: HarperCollins.

Gordon, S. (2005). *Guess who spins.* New York: Benchmark/Marshall Cavendish.

Harris, R. (1999). *It's so amazing!: A book about eggs, sperm, birth, babies, and families.* Cambridge, MA: Candlewick.

Henkes, K. (2003). *Olive's ocean.* New York: Greenwillow/HarperCollins.

Hoffman, K. (in press). Professional ethics in librarianship. *Texas Library Journal.*

The Horn Book Guide. (2005). 16 (1), 126-127.

Horvath, P. (2005). *The Pepins and their problems.* New York: Farrar.

Lockhart, D. (1996). Self-Censorship in Elementary School Librarians, Master's Paper, Texas Woman's University: Denton Texas.

Loertscher, D. (1988). *Taxonomies of the school library media program.* Englewood, CO: Libraries Unlimited.

Montgomery, S. (2004). *The tarantula scientist*. Boston: Houghton Mifflin.

Murawski, D. (2004). *Spiders and their webs*. Washington, DC: National Geographic Society.

Paulsen, G. (1988). *Hatchet*. New York: Viking.

Price, A., & Yaakov, J. (2001). *Children's catalog* (18th ed.). New York: The H. W. Wilson Company.

Price, A., Yaakov, J., & Padró, Z. N. (Eds.). (2000). *Middle and junior high school library catalog* (8th ed.). New York: The H. W. Wilson Company.

Simot, M. (2001). *The stray dog*. New York: HarperCollins.

Sutton, R. (2005). Telephone interview with Betty Carter, June 21.

St. Lifer, E. (2005). 2005 book prices. *School Library Journal, 51*(3), 11.

TitleWave. Last accessed August 2005 at http://www.flr.follett.com/

Towsend, J. (2005). *Incredible arachnids*. Austin, TX: Raintree/Steck-Vaughn.

The world book encyclopedia. World Book, Field Enterprises.

World Cultures Today. Last accessed July 2005 at http://www.greenwood.com/worldculturestoday

Yaakov, J. (Ed.). (2002). *Senior high school library catalog* (16th ed.). New York: The H. W. Wilson Company.

Additional Resources

Booklist, published twice monthly September through June and monthly in July and August by the American Library Association, 50 E. Huron Street, Chicago, IL 60611

Bulletin of the Center for Children's Books, published monthly except August by Johns Hopkins University Press for the Graduate School of Library and Information Science at the University of Illinois at Urbana-Champlain.

The Horn Book Guide, published quarterly by Horn Book Inc., 56 Roland Street, Suite 200, Boston, Massachusetts 02129.

The Horn Book Magazine, published bimonthly by Horn Book Inc., 56 Roland Street, Suite 200, Boston, Massachusetts 02129.

School Library Journal, published monthly by Reed Business Information, 360 Park Avenue South, New York, New York 10010.

Voice of Youth Advocates (VOYA), published bimonthly by Scarecrow Press, 4501 Forbes Blvd., Suite 200, Lanham, Maryland 20706.

CHAPTER FIVE:
FINANCIAL SUPPORT and LIBRARY PROGRAMS

Jim Hundemer

There is no doubt that a quality library program, properly funded, staffed, equipped, and taught can make all the difference to a school community and to a district overall. The tough part is for the library director to convey that message and more importantly to "lead" that message to actual implementation. The director must clearly understand the end goal, be able to recognize it at each stage of implementation (which can be five years down the road), and be prepared to handle each and every roadblock as well as opportunity that didn't exist when you started—some anticipated, some out of the clear blue sky. In a five-year period you can have a change in administration in Washington and at least two regular sessions of the state legislature, all impacting the library's goals and plans. About the worse thing that could happen is that there is a change in superintendents during this time, and the process must be restarted. If you are at the beginning of this process then it may not make any difference if the superintendent changes. The director must never lose focus and keep his/her eye on the prize.

Developing goals and plans can never be done in isolation. Invite librarians to join in consultation on a regular basis to review your ideas and add ideas of their own that you believe will enhance the end product. Invite selected principals to join you in a "Principal's Advisory Group" and share your vision with them and seek their input. Share your plans with as many people and organizations as you can. You must become very visible. Go to PTA/PTO meetings and seek input and help. Share your goals and plans with the board of the public library if there is a relationship between the public library system and the school district. That relationship can be simply that the public libraries fill up with your kids when school is out, and if there isn't one, create one. Involve yourself in assisting with the public libraries' summer reading programs. During this time you will refine, refine, and re-refine your product.

The library director cannot approach the superintendent for financial support without credibility. If you do many of the things discussed here, the word will begin to get around that there is this person that thinks he or she has a chance to change things. You and your program need to be as visible as possible, of course, in a positive way. If your community has cable access for education, develop a television series dedicated to your school library program. Showcase school programs, librarians, and kids. If you are in the midst of renovation and construction, do a show on library makeovers and what is new at the library. And of course, develop programs around the project and what must be done. Interview upper level administrators about projects they are working on that impact reading in the district. Show how the library program will support what they are trying to do. Student contests such as Name That Book or Battle of the Books are another great way to gain visibility. Always showcase the very youngest students, the K-2 contestants. Invite the local television station out for the finals. Be certain that you get pictures on your Web site and to all the local papers. Anything you can think of to draw positive images of the library program will reap benefits to your leadership and hopefully, your budget.

It is also important for the library director to clearly understand the budgeting process. You must know how the overall budget process works—who controls the decisions at each level. You must know how capital projects like you are proposing are generally funded. If the state allows a district to divert a portion of the tax rate for capital projects then make that your suggestion on how the program will be funded. We all understand that the superintendent and the school board must approve everything on a large scale, but the people in place who will take all of this forward are key to success. The timeframes in which they operate are vital to your success. It is important to keep in mind that you are asking the superintendent to give your plan special consideration since funds will have to be redirected or new sources found to fund it. You also need to find out who the other departments are that also have goals, plans, and visions as well. You network, network, and network. Attend as many principal's meetings as you can, also district meetings where you share your goals and plans and then stay to hear what else they are up to and what ideas they have to offer. When you attend your own reporting structure staff meetings, take notes on all those with special projects on the table. Try and enlist as many of these individuals to see the value of what you are doing and explore ways you can work together. And say to yourself constantly, "Why should the superintendent pick my project over all these others that stand to improve the lives of children as well?"

Building Your Case

So you want your reporting structure, your supervisor's reporting structure, the superintendent, and the school board to say "yes" to your "quality school library program." Build your case and present it to your supervisor. You must have data and proof that you can change things. There are lots of ways to get data and here are a couple that have worked for me. I had software analysis done on the "best" schools in the district and also some of the neediest. If you break it down by subject category, you can show that at the "best" schools science materials and nonfiction are woefully out of date. It will create a strong point for your case. Build the case for every district/area/region within your school system. Your book vendors can help you with this. It is also helpful if you can find data from contiguous school districts as well as those that have quality library programs around the state.

The equity issue is always there for you to use, but you have to be careful. Look at other projects that used it in the past and see what the reaction was. If the powers that be don't want it acknowledged, do it in subtle ways. Focus on all schools. Show that as a district everyone can come together and benefit from what you are trying to do and the equity issue will take care of itself. There is a lot to say about being positive. Never refer to your predecessor or how it "used" to be. Take the high road. Only speak about how much better it will be for all kids when your plan is implemented.

As part of building your case, you should find some examples of outdated materials throughout your system. Have a weeding contest. Create categories like the oldest, most mold (sent in Ziploc bags), most worn, most politically incorrect title, oldest last check-out date, most stained, most chewed up, most creative student enhanced illustrations, and the books with the most out-of-date information. Keep it funny and while everyone is laughing you will have gotten a valuable message across, and you may see the books used by the superintendent to make his case to the public in a press conference.

Certainly, if your state has standards by which libraries are measured and assessed then they would be used to show how your district stacks up. In my experience, most schools fail when compared to state standards, even the "best of the best." That message often falls on deaf ears, but if the comparative data can help, certainly use it. If all schools fail then I probably wouldn't use it since it points out what everyone already knows. If the results are mixed then consider using it, but only show that with support you will focus first on those schools that need the most help.

If you still need additional data, develop a survey of your own librarians that will help your case using many of the categories from the state standards, but also specific categories such as budget for library materials on each campus, the automation system used if it is not centralized, the age of the current software, circulation statistics, and technology available for student use.

Putting It Together and Presenting Your Plan

You will need at least three versions of your plan for presentation. The first plan must be a very detailed plan for library professionals and supporters as well as first level administrators—your direct report. This plan will also serve as the foundation for upper level presentations, but they will be much shorter. The third version should be a 15- to 30-minute presentation for the superintendent—that is all the time you will likely get to convince her to fund your plan. You should always have with you pertinent details that you can recall at a moment's notice in case you are stopped and asked specific questions.

Regardless of the current unpopularity with using PowerPoint presentations, it is the easiest way for you to stay focused when presenting to various groups that will constantly interrupt you with questions. The down side is making sure that all of the equipment is in place and *working* each time you make the presentation. Get used to carrying backups of everything. It will force you to make arrangements with the meeting host to visit the presentation room in advance and assess the facility for your presentation. When preparing for your presentation consider: size of the room and the projection screen, location of the podium/conference table, usual seating arrangements used for the meeting room, electrical outlets, and the PA system. You must make arrangements to get the room setup well before the meeting and plan to test the facility and rehearse your presentation. Always be prepared with plan B. Have a print version of your plan that you will be able to walk participants through in the event you cannot get into the facility in advance, you are not given enough time to set up, or some equipment does not work. You should rehearse your plan B just as much as the PowerPoint presentation.

The PowerPoint presentation should contain all of the detail that you will need for the various audiences that you are presenting to. You can always skip over screens that seem irrelevant to the group before you, but it is amazing how often you will use them when questions come up. The first half of the presentation will show the "problem," and it should contain all of the data that you have gathered and clearly displayed to show the need for what you will propose. The second half of the presentation will show your plan for solving the problem and can be further subdivided into multiple year solutions. In other words, you show what will happen in year 1 through year 4 if that is how long it will take you to implement your plan. Spreading your implementation plan out over several budget years helps in several ways. The superintendent will not have to come up with a huge amount of money all at once and if your plan involves a large school district you wouldn't be able to get it done in one year anyway. So to make sure you get it done correctly and avoid chaos and inconsistency, spread the implementation piece out over several years. You will become very popular with all the principals that want to be in the first year of implementation, and you will also have plenty of principals that will want to wait until year four.

Your presentation should not last longer than 45 minutes and with whatever balance of time is given by the host of the meeting for questions. Shorter is better. Prior to your presentation or after you have finished you should "work the room." Shake hands with everyone that is in the room and thank them for their time. If you have an opportunity to see any of them again at other functions or in the lunchroom, try and engage them about how they feel about what you are trying to do, and then ask them about their "grandbabies." You should have some testimonials ready to go for any occasion. "I was at a school library and was watching some students that appeared to be doing research. I approached them and asked what they were working on, and they said a report on the history of computers. One of the books they were using had a copyright date of 1968." And another, "Mr. Superintendent, if all of the children in the school district could read on grade level, most of our problems would go away." And, " The only way to grow readers is sustained reading. The library program grows readers." Phrases like these are what people will remember about what you are trying to do.

Now it is time to present your plan to the superintendent. This can be three years after you first put your ideas on paper, but it is show time! Your plan will have evolved naturally over that time, and it will have evolved with all the input you have received since you began presenting it. Just keep two things in mind. Number one is that the superintendent has four other presentations after yours all asking to fund some new idea that will improve the district in some way, and second, his or her motivation for approving your plan may not be your motivation, which is a quality library program. So don't seem surprised that a press officer is in the room taking notes to see how the district can get a positive "spin" out of what you are trying to do. The superintendent may want to get other departments involved with your plan. Don't get so attached to your plan that you can't compromise and make accommodations. You will need to work with other departments anyway, such as technology, to get the plan implemented.

If you intend to write library curriculum, certainly the curriculum department belongs at the table. If the superintendent asks for your best thinking on an issue or concern give a positive response. Try and move your opinions in the direction that you see that the superintendent is going. If there are multiple levels of your reporting structure in the room, let them help sell your program. If you have gotten to a meeting with the superintendent, your reporting structure is convinced that what you are doing is worthwhile. Try not to talk over anyone who is singing your plan's praises. You usually won't have to do all the talking. Listening and strategizing can be very useful. There are usually four things that the superintendent will look at and they are your plan, its need, how that need fits in with the overall plans in the district, and the amount of money you want. The budget, which will be addressed next, is usually not an issue because the superintendent trusts that the amount of money you want for a new automation system is accurate. What will be critical is the timeline you have prepared for implementation and how the funds will be spread out over time, and where the money will come from.

Do not leave the meeting with the superintendent without clearly understanding any modifications that he has requested and a timeline for you to get that information back to him. Also never leave the meeting without a "next step" process date and time even if it's meeting with the press officer to schedule a press conference. Also never leave the meeting without clearly noting all the instructions he has given everyone else that is at the meeting. You will need to follow up with each one of them to gently remind them of what needs to be done, and that you will get most of the leg work done for them. And most importantly, thank everyone who has been a part of getting you this far. You might even come up with some special item to show your appreciation.

The Budget

It might seem odd that the discussion of the development of the budget comes after the presentation to the superintendent, but it is about the least important part of the whole process. If your plan shows a clear need and you articulate the plan well and are able to convince an entire administration that it is something that is in the vital interests of all children in the system, then you will be trusted to get the numbers right. The administration will not understand union catalogs, retrospective conversion fees, catalog administrator, MARC records software, online resources, and other musts for a quality library program. So develop a budget that allows you to stretch the funds out over no more than four years and create a narrative that explains which pieces of the budget will occur in year one and why, and continue this through years three and four. Develop objectives and outcomes for each of the years to be funded. You should take your budget to someone in the budget office and share the information so you can be sure that you have thought of everything. At the budget office ask how capital projects such as the one you are proposing are funded, and ask the budget officer to share with you all the ways that it has happened in the recent past. Find out if there are state laws or rules that give you special consideration for funding sources. In many states the law allows a school district to use a portion of the tax rate to fund special projects—such as a library upgrade project—for definite periods of time. So after you have calculated the total amount of funds needed for your project, you should be able to make a request that makes sense and shows that the overall effect of your project on the district budget will not be that significant. Just ask for a "penny" of the tax rate if, when calculated out, it will fund your project. If it takes two pennies then so be it. Rather than asking for $9 million from the superintendent, it would be better to say, "Mr. Superintendent we are only asking for 2 cents of the tax rate over a four-year period." Whenever you make a presentation to anyone on your budget use this figure not $9 million. However you decide to do your calculations, using percentages of total budgets is more effective and less painful to the administrators and the school board who have to say "yes." How can they not fund a quality school library program, the Heart of Every School, when it will cost just two cents of the tax rate? "Well, of course, we can afford that," they will all say!

When you implement your budget, you will have the most schools to upgrade in the first year. These will be the schools that have a good program, know what you want to accomplish, and will be ready to move once the project is approved. So budget appropriately. Years two through four will be your toughest years.

As a part of the budgeting process it is time to think about doubling your money. You can do this by asking principals, at whose schools you plan to expend your funds, to match a dollar amount. For example, you provide $10,000 for books from your budget and the principal must match that amount. Or, if you are installing telephone tech lines, the librarian could pay for the installation and the principal pays the monthly fees. Or, the library budget pays for two computers and the principal supports the program with two more. You get the idea. Just remember to ask for these kinds of commitments up front since it will be very hard to get them after the fact. Also when the superintendent and school board sign on to your plan it makes the commitments "official."

We all know that a quality library program is also defined by a flexible scheduling plan that allows librarians time to collaborate with teachers on lesson plans. Once your plan is approved you have an opportunity to negotiate that as well. Make a list of all the things you plan to provide each school and note the value of it, and then ask for a flexible schedule for your librarians as a condition of participation in the plan. This is for those school districts that operate in a decentralized environment, where one often finds a variety of librarian schedules throughout the system. If you see that asking for this is not tenable, then negotiate it by offering your fully funded plan for a 60/40 flexible schedule plan or some version of this number. In the 60/40 plan the librarian would be in the flexible schedule 60 percent of the instructional day and 40 percent in ancillary rotation or covering classes. If you think you might have trouble with the principals on any of this, enlist the support of the superintendent. Unless the principal is a former librarian, most of them will not understand how important a quality library program can be to their overall test scores and student achievement. Once they begin to put their own funds in the program they will pay attention to it. They will ask the librarian questions and pay attention to a librarian quarterly report (which all librarians should be doing) a little more closely than would otherwise be the case. It will also set the groundwork for the librarian to approach the principal for new funds and equipment replacement funds once the project has been completed.

Conversely, if the librarian is not carrying his or her weight and things are not going well in the library, the principal may opt not to add anything to the program. You must have at least a minimum level of service and equipment to all schools or the students in that school will suffer. Of course your real goal should be to exceed the minimum level of service. Each year you should provide your direct supervisor and the superintendent with a progress report on the implementation of the program. Be careful not to share a report showing a list of all principals and the amount matched with nothing in the columns for those that did not offer a match or simply a list of principals not matching the funds. You should try the positive approach first with the list of "all" principals, and provide district totals so the superintendent can see how significantly schools are participating in your project. The numbers the first year will be quite impressive. The negative aspect of the report will take care of itself. When principals complain at a principal's meeting with the superintendent that they need money, it can be pointed out they had an opportunity to match funds with the library program and they failed to take advantage of the opportunity.

Now You Have Your Program—What's Next?

If you were not high profile before, your funded project put you in the limelight. Make sure to never give up that spotlight! Every time you go to a principals' meeting there will be a dozen principals that will pull you aside and "thank you" for all the great things that you have done for their libraries and they will then ask you for something else. Do your best to accommodate their requests. If you were not involved at certain meetings before your project began, you now will be and you must take the opportunity, if asked, to let them know how it is going. Have the numbers memorized so you can give a 10-minute report on the spot. That should include total dollars spent, total computers and other technology added for kids, total number of books purchased, and if the test scores in reading are up, take some credit for that as well. Present you message at every opportunity. The library board of the public library, the Friends group of the local library, and PTA/PTO meetings are just some venues for you to celebrate your program. The reason these groups and others like them are so important is that most of the time they are activists and leaders in the community. At events they host with your superintendent your name may come up as someone who is making a difference in the school district, and your program will become even more highly visible. If asked to serve on other committees involving other aspects of school business, you should eagerly volunteer. Share this work with your consensus groups and come to some conclusions on how the library program can contribute. Where it is feasible, weave the library program throughout every aspect of the district.

It is time for you to begin working on the next part of "growing your library program." Start at the beginning with consensus groups and work it all over again. You will have an easier time of it since you are now a proven quantity in the district. The day you sit back and say that you have accomplished all that you started out to accomplish will be the first day of the beginning of the decline in your district library program.

It Will All Collapse without Training

Changing the library program on any scale will fail without adequate training. The larger the project, the more training is needed to guarantee success. One of the aspects of principal participation in your project must be an agreement to release the librarian for training. You may even want to quantify the actual hours required and what will be taught, such as Library Automation Product I, II, and III, each requiring two hours or a half-day—whatever it takes, but everyone should know up front what is required for success. For large projects you need to budget for a full-time person such as a systems manager or technologist to handle implementation. Once the librarians have been through all the training, offer training to teachers and administrators on other non-librarian aspects such as online resources. Bring them to your computer lab and greet each person and welcome them to your facility and thank them for going back to their schools and sharing their training with others. Make sure you offer training during and after school hours and on Saturdays. As long as there are employees of your district willing to give their time to understand what you have to offer, you must be there to offer it. Every year you should make arrangements to present at the "New Teacher Orientation" meeting and if break-out sessions are offered, you should certainly be prepared to present one. Have brochures printed with all the information they need to get started, such as suggestions for using the library, Web addresses for all their online resources, and anything else you think new teachers need. Be sure and pass the new teachers' names on to your librarians so that they will bring them into the library for a personal orientation. And, of course, you must provide at least a full day of orientation for new school librarians.

There isn't a more critical group to win to your side than principals. With all the heavy responsibilities that their jobs entail you must do everything you can to accommodate them and help them. If your librarian assessment instrument is different than regular teachers, you should offer training on it just for them. Bring them to a library facility for half-day. Begin with a nice breakfast or lunch and then personally welcome each one and thank them for attending. Of course, you will offer a brief overview of all that your department has done, and you will quote the numbers you have memorized. Most of the principals attending this type of training will be relatively new so take the opportunity to "grow them" as library friendly. Give them interview questions and techniques for hiring a librarian. Share with them what they should see as they do a "walk through" of the library. Volunteer to come out or send a staff member out to look at doing a "library makeover." Then proceed to train them on the instrument.

Many large districts will actually have "New Principal Institutes" where all the new principals and assistant principals will come together once a month to learn various aspects of district operations. Make sure you get on the agenda for a minimum of a half-day or two half-days. On the second half-day ask them to return to the meeting with their librarian and a floor plan of the library. During the first half of the training have a "New Principal Library Manual" ready for each participant. It should contain items such as state library standards, credentials and course preparations required of librarians, information on selecting a librarian, a brief description of cataloging and classification, information on the library automation system the district uses, library facility evaluation and design, the district library program and curriculum integration—to include the library's roll in state tests, and finally, the librarian appraisal system. During the next meeting the librarian and new principal will work together to set goals for the year—a process that will continue every year and should include how to budget a library program and a review of the facility itself with suggestions for improving its operation and attractiveness. One of the main problems that library programs face is having a principal that has had little or no experience in dealing with one of the most expensive and important facilities in the school building. Principal preparation classes at universities have seldom offered any courses dealing with the complexities of managing a quality library program, so it is up to the library director.

Just as most of you get visibility with your Librarian of the Year recognition you should also have a Principal of the Year program. Choose one from the elementary schools and one from secondary. Have the librarians send their nominations to you and then you can put together a committee to screen them. Once the selection is made, make sure you get on the agenda of the principals' meeting to showcase that principal in front of other principals and the superintendent. It would even be better if you could offer prizes such as $1,000 worth of free books for their library or a new computer for students to use in the library in addition to the nice plaque or trophy.

And, of Course, All Your Librarians Are Perfect

The most difficult aspect of library director leadership in getting budgets for the program is dealing with personnel. A lot of the problems you will encounter with principals have to do with what was discussed earlier—principals don't really understand how a library works and the role it and the librarian should play in every aspect of school activity. If you are viewed as a leader by the principals, then they will want to discuss problems about their librarians with you even if you have no direct role in assessing them. And here you will become a "matchmaker." Most often librarians want to do the best job they can, but what they perceive as the job and what the principals perceive can be two completely different things. Personalities are a huge part of this. Get to know your librarians and their histories as well as the principals. Do your best to make the match that will put the two together that can work together. Most often this is doing what the principal wants. Generally, if you make the match, budgets will also get better for the program and it will reflect on your leadership. Just when you think a principal is beyond salvation in building a library program, you will find the match that turns the entire thing around. However, there will be some that you just have to wait out their retirement if you can't get either one to budge, but most people long for a pleasant and happy work environment. And of course, you will need to support those principals when their librarian is one of those … just there to get out of the classroom! Nothing is happening in the library. It is a dismal place and the students will tell you they do not want to go in there, and teachers feel the same way. You have to support the principal in moving that librarian on. One of the ways to make sure you are right in backing the principal is to share your concerns with the librarian and let her know that you are going to do a survey of teachers and students about the library and its use. If the results come back as expected you must support the principal in putting the librarian on a one-year growth plan, and if progress is not made you must support termination. If on the other hand the results support the librarian, you should assist the librarian in finding another position at the end of the school year. These are tough calls especially when you are not on the campus everyday, but a strong library director must make them. It will lead to a stronger program and better budgets across time.

Finally, Go Looking for More Money

Now that you know the process to make everyone happy and to fund the best library program, sustainability is the operative word. Certainly, you should now move to a continuation budget that sustains what you have put in place. Use new collection analysis reports that show the progress you have made, but clearly show more needs to be done. By the end of your three- or four-year program, many of the computers will need to be replaced. If that flex plan begins to wobble a little bit, go for an injunction from the superintendent and school board. Your new library program has generated all kinds of excitement in the district and the workload for the librarians has doubled; it is now time to ask for clerical support for all of your libraries. You can justify it!

You must become a state and federal grant expert. There are plenty of grant opportunities to support what you are trying to do. If your district has a grant department, become their new best friend if you are not already. If you don't know how to write a grant and the school district can't help you, there are a lot of grant writing books and consultants around to help you. Even single school grants are worth the effort and will reflect on your leadership, but every so often you will get the big one—a new computer for each and every one of your 300 schools!

CHAPTER SIX: COLLABORATION

Mary Frances Long

Look carefully at the word "collaboration." In the middle of the word you see an extremely important word—labor. As a teacher-librarian, you need to understand that in order to cultivate strong collaborative relationships with the learning community on your campus, you will need to continuously work to expand and strengthen your skills and abilities.

Work to develop new advocates for your school library program and work to nurture and maintain the advocates you have gained. There is no time to rest on your laurels.

Collaborative Work Is Never Done

Why does it take continual work on your part to develop and maintain collaborative relationships with your stakeholders? Think about it. The administrators, parents, students, and most importantly the teachers, who are all members of the learning community, are not static. Administrators come and go. Current administrators leave or retire, making room for new principals and assistant principals who are hired or reassigned to your campus. Parents and their children move through your campus as students progress through their years of education. Teachers are frequently moving across grade levels, into different or new departments or campuses.

Some of your stakeholders appreciate and value teacher-librarians as contributing educators to student academic achievement and place a high value on school library programs. Some come to your campus with negative perspectives based on their experiences with predecessors who may not have worked so hard to build a relationship with them. Some stakeholders simply do not know and understand what school libraries and the professionals who manage them can contribute to improving student academic achievement. More than likely you will find a compilation of positive and negative perspectives regarding you as a professional educator and whether the school library program is valued as a dynamic student-center aspect of the academic environment on your campus.

You need to remember that strong collaborative relationships are the best means for integrating the library program into the school curriculum. Whatever you do, working on strengthening your relationships with your stakeholders is one way of eliminating the isolation many teacher-librarians experience. By working as a dynamic curriculum and instructional leader on the campus you are strengthening the library program's connections to stakeholders and improving your relationship with them as well.

Information Power Sets the Stage

Information Power: Building Partnerships for Learning (1998), the publication published by American Association of School Librarians (AASL) and Association for Educational Communication and Technology (AECT), is founded on the themes of collaboration, technology, and leadership. The 1998 standards and principles for school libraries do not indicate what element of the three is most important. Depending on a person's interests and strengths, if asked, the elements would be ranked in order of importance differently from person to person. What does remain hard and fast is the fact that teacher-librarians must develop good leadership and collaboration skills to be effective on their campuses.

After his review of statewide studies that addressed the impact of school library media centers on academic achievement, Lance (2003) found that although collaboration is emphasized over leadership, *Information Power* studies "indicate that leadership's impact on academic achievement is the prime mover behind collaboration with teachers" (AASL & AECT, 1998, p. 90). Lance found that when teacher-librarians function as leaders on their campuses, collaboration increases and teaching opportunities in the library and in the classroom occur more often.

Although collaboration is a necessary vital element in developing a strong library, leadership skills are the key to successfully implementing and infusing the library program into the curriculum. The librarian's ability to exercise strong curricular and instructional leadership complements the abilities of taking the lead as an advocate for information literacy. This serves in strengthening and improving collaborative relationships with your stakeholders. Work to develop new advocates for the library program and work to nurture and maintain the ones you have gained. There is no time to rest on your laurels.

Influence Through Leadership

As already stated, leadership is one of the three themes given strong emphasis and acknowledgement in *Information Power*. Leadership is cited together with collaboration and technology. All three ideas/themes are necessary in developing a dynamic library program, but in order for you to establish effective collaborative relationships with your staff and administrators, it is essential for you to develop a level of influence on your campus. The level of influence that the librarian acquires is dependent on the effort you apply in being a pivotal leader in your school community.

Remember, you have the ability to become an indispensable educational leader. If you do not step forward, offering support and forming alliances with your stakeholders, your knowledge of the curriculum, your expertise in information literacy, and the far reaching potential of the contributions you can make to the learning community, will not become known or valued.

You must be a leader who is willing to face challenges head on. In order to accomplish your mission, you must be a leader who works to improve professional credibility and to gain acceptance from all of your stakeholders: administrators, parents, principals, school board members, and most importantly teachers.

Leadership Is Learnable

It is extremely important at this point to clear up a misconception. No matter what you have heard, leaders—are not born. Leadership skills are not innate, but must be developed and nurtured based on sound foundations and understandings. More importantly, you must believe that the leadership abilities of the professional teacher-librarian are a key factor in developing a strong and successful library program.

People who are leaders learn, adapt, and improve their leadership style and skills by thinking and acting like leaders. You can continue to develop and improve your leadership skills by reading books on leadership, attending courses on being a leader, and by thinking, believing, and functioning like a leader.

Of course, you may not be considered a formal leader on your campus, like your principal and other administrators, but there are many ways you can function like a leader informally by serving on building- and district-level committees. Your informal leadership can be strengthened by your willingness to work on campus-related activities that do not directly tie into the library program, but rest assured your efforts will not go unnoticed. Search for ways to strengthen your stakeholders' perception of you as a leader. Be creative and willing to be adventurous.

Think of yourself as a leader from the middle who has the formidable responsibility of earning and sustaining credibility among your stakeholders. Think of yourself as the leader who must forge alliances with your stakeholders in order for you to be seen as an educational leader who manages an indispensable educational facility.

Today, educational systems must look to every member of their learning community to function as leaders and these same educational systems encourage every member to think like a leader. All leaders, whether they are formally installed in leadership position or as the librarian who has the opportunity to function in an informal leadership role, have something to contribute to the overall success of their organization. You, as the teacher-librarian on your campus, have many opportunities to practice and hone leadership skills. First and foremost, you must work to demonstrate your expertise in your roles as information specialist, teacher, program administrator, and instructional partner by assuming the responsibility of encouraging a culture of collaboration throughout your learning community.

The Labor of Collaborating

As a teacher-librarian who is working toward developing strong collaborative relationships with your learning community, you will need to take the lead in initiating and promoting collaboration with your stakeholders. Your leadership abilities, your efforts to develop a collaborative environment, and your level of skill will all prove vital in your role as an instructional partner.

In order to improve your collaborative relationships, you have to work closely with a variety of members of the school's learning community, our stakeholders. You must be able to make this collaborative relationship work. As the educator who is functioning as the "Lone Ranger" in charge of the library program, it is important to understand your role as instructional partner and know how to promote yourself and the library program to your stakeholders. Remember your collaboration efforts are vital in developing a rich learning environment for your students.

The Choice Is Yours

Information Power utilizes the words lead, leader, and leadership a multitude of times in describing the roles and responsibilities of teacher-librarians (AASL & AECT, 1998). The standards and principles written in the 1998 edition propose a daunting list of responsibilities for teacher-librarians. You can choose to perceive your roles and responsibilities as a burden, but a better option is to consider them as the means to ensure the stated mission of an effective school library program is accomplished. Your mission, if you choose to accept it, is to "ensure that students and staff are effective users of ideas and information" (AASL & AECT, 1998, p. 6).

In order to accomplish your mission, your collaboration efforts depend on your personality and your interpersonal skills to help you along. To be a leader, you must foster relationships, trust, and influence. You must be willing to take risks and be innovative. You must demonstrate your expertise as a school librarian, as detailed in *Information Power,* while also functioning as a teacher. The choice is yours.

Works Cited

American Association of School Librarians, & Association for Educational Communications and Technology. (1998). *Information power: Building partnerships for learning.* Chicago: American Library Association.

Lance, K.C., & Loertscher, D. V. (2003). *Powering achievement: School library media programs make a difference: The evidence mounts.* San Jose, CA: Hi Willow.

CHAPTER SEVEN: PROFESSIONAL DEVELOPMENT

Mary Beth Green

Imagine, for a moment, that there was a doctor who believed that everything that was important to know about medicine was taught in medical school. At the beginning, he was considered to be at the top of the field. However, as time passed, new drugs were discovered. New treatments for disease were found. Old methods were found to be inadequate. All of this new information was disregarded by our physician as unnecessary or not consistent with what he had learned in school. Some of his patients got better, but many of his patients never seemed to respond to treatment. "If only," thought the doctor, "they would listen to me more carefully and follow my instructions." Eventually, patients began falling away and started seeking help from other doctors whose knowledge and skills were more current.

Educators viewing this scenario would be shocked. They would call the doctor's behavior "reckless," "arrogant," or even "dangerous." When pressed for an explanation, most would proclaim, "People's lives are at stake." Shift the focus to education. Supposing the doctor is now a library media specialist. Frequently, library media specialists burdened with wearying schedules view professional development as a waste of time. Ironically, we view professional development as vital to the outcome of the doctor's patients' lives, yet we don't make that same connection to the outcomes for our students. Shouldn't we hold the same expectations for ourselves as library media specialists as we do for doctors?

Our schools are facing increasingly demanding challenges. Recent years have witnessed a clarion call for boosting student performance in public education. Students face ever increasing expectations and must meet rigorous standards throughout their school careers. Concurrently, what educators are expected to know and do has increased in amount and complexity (NECTL, 1994). At the same time, our schools are becoming more culturally, ethnically, and linguistically diverse. Just when we need a highly trained cadre of educators, many educators tend to gravitate back to the same methods by which they were taught (Sparks & Hirsch, 1997).

Many library media specialists would agree that professional development is one of the most powerful strategies in bringing about the changes necessary to improve student learning. Yet, mention the words "professional development" and many would roll their eyes. This is not surprising in light of the fact that much of what has passed as professional development in the past has failed to deliver the same quality of instruction for educators that is demanded for students

No longer, though, can library media specialist view professional development as something that must simply be endured. In order to serve schools facing a multitude of challenges, library media specialists must not only develop deep understandings of information literacy, but also of the content domains that they serve. Library media specialists will only gain credibility with other faculty, if they have a clear, up-to-date understanding of current learning theories, pedagogy, and can create concrete links from the information sciences to those content domains that enable student success.

A strong library media program draws on the rich background of the library media specialist and provides numerous opportunities for professional development for the faculty. Professional development for faculty, provided by the library media specialist, serves the dual purpose of enriching faculty knowledge and skills as well as establishing the library media specialist as school leader. Ultimately, research shows that strong leadership by the library media specialist is linked to student achievement (Hamilton-Pennell, Lance, Rodney, & Hainer, 2000). The purpose of this chapter is to:

- *examine the concept of professional development;*
- *review characteristics of effective professional development programs;*
- *discuss the variety of professional development approaches;*
- *explore the process of evaluation; and*
- *provide suggestions for planning an effective professional development program.*

Simply stated, professional development is defined as "those processes and activities designed to enhance the professional knowledge, skills and attitudes of educators so that they might, in turn, improve the learning of students" (Guskey, 2000, p. 16). Further, Sparks & Hirsch (1997) assert that professional development is "a means to an end rather than an end in itself; it helps educators close the gap between current practices and the practices needed to achieve the desired outcomes" (p. 24). Loucks-Horsley et al. (1987) suggest that successful professional development is a process, not an event.

Professional Development Best Practices

Numerous researchers, professional organizations, and theorists have examined the concept of professional development from a variety of perspectives. There is general consensus that professional development anchored in several key elements, enables educator learning that supports student performance. Drawing from constructivism and adult learning theory, these principles create environments that support learning and empower educators to reach their true potential. These elements include:

> A) *drawing from a coherent vision or plan for professional development,*
>
> B) *using student data when making decisions about content,*
>
> C) *encouraging collaborative partnerships,*
>
> D) *providing opportunities for reflection,*
>
> E) *incorporating opportunities for active learning, and*
>
> F) *sustaining learning over time with follow-up support and programs.*

Coherent Vision

Too often, a school's professional development program offers a disjointed agenda. The yearly sequence of in-service days makes awkward twists and turns into new pedagogies, classroom management strategies, and bonding experiences. While each of these activities has value, as a collection they do not present a well thought-out, coherent vision for educator learning leading to student success.

Successful districts and schools maintain a coherent vision for school improvement over time. Faculties in these districts have a clear understanding of what students should know and be able to do. The vision provides a common direction focusing efforts on the stated mission of the school or district. Professional development programs in these districts and schools are guided by this common vision. New pedagogies, classroom management strategies, and even bonding experiences are interwoven into this system of professional development as part of a cohesive effort to achieve the vision.

Enabling this vision should become the essential goal for the librarians and the library staff. There are several points at which the library program and the coherent vision should intersect. First, the librarian should be involved in creating the coherent vision or plan for student success at either the district or school level. As the information resource for the school, the library department will need to plan for the resources or services that the new plan will require. Second, librarians should be actively involved in the implementation of the vision. This may mean attending training in order to fully understand any underlying philosophies or new pedagogies. Third, the library should look for programs, activities, or resources provided by the library that can visibly support the plan. Finally, professional development provided by the library department for faculty should connect to the vision.

Data Driven Content

In the past, the choice of content for professional development was guided by fads, trends, or quick fixes. Typically, topics for professional development would be based on what seemed to be working at another school or on what someone had heard about at a conference. These activities frequently had only a loose connection to any school or district goal. Although teachers gained new skills, this new learning rarely impacted the underlying problems facing educators in their school environment. Student performance, the ultimate goal for professional development, was only faintly impacted.

Today, educators recognize that effective professional development must be tightly targeted to student needs. Many educators recognize that to promote success for students, professional development must address those areas of difference between student performance and goals and standards for student learning. By analyzing these data sources, educators are learning where students need stronger support and educators need to refine their practice. Although student scores on standardized tests are the most frequent source of data, numerous other data sources are available such as AP test scores, graduation rates, and end of course exams. Professional development for and by library media specialists should incorporate this paradigm.

- *First, it is vital that library media specialists take part in campus and district meetings where results of student performance are analyzed. Taking part in these discussions ensures that library media specialists are not only aware of the areas needing attention, but also enables them to begin finding strategies to support both teachers and students.*

- *Second, in order to understand goals and standards for student performance, library media specialists should take advantage of opportunities to become familiar with the curriculum frameworks that are in place in their state.*

- *Third, professional development for library media specialists should not simply focus on the newest database or circulation system reports, but should also address how these innovations support student learning within the curriculum frameworks and especially identified student weaknesses.*

- *Fourth, when delivering professional development, a knowledgeable library media specialist will connect library services to the curriculum frameworks and the goals and standards for student learning. Teachers burdened with large classes and heavy responsibilities may view library technologies and innovations as nice additions, but may not see the relevance of these to their curricular needs unless the library media specialist can concretely make the connections.*

Collaborative Model

Norms of isolation and autonomy are deeply embedded in American education. Traditional approaches to professional development emphasize private, individual activity, and are rooted in the belief that the individual teacher is responsible for the problems of education (Shroyer, 1990). The deficit model informs this approach, where administrators perceive deficits in each teacher's knowledge that must be corrected. Teacher learning and improvement, thus, become an individual responsibility (Smylie & Conyers, 1991). Teacher interactions in traditional professional development workshops tend to be "brief and casual" with few "active, ongoing exchanges of ideas and practices" (Goodlad 1984, p. 187). This problem is reinforced by structural and cultural restraints on communication between teachers including cellular classrooms, individualized teaching assignments, and occupational norms of personal autonomy (Little, 1992).

Providing time for collaboration and communication is essential to generating powerful shared learning (Darling-Hammond, 1998). Drawing from social cognitive theory, which asserts that people learn from their social environments (Schunk, 2000), communication and collaboration help educators foster a better understanding of the goals for student learning through sharing methods, discussing written work, and reflecting on problems and solutions (Garet, Porter, Desimone, Birman, & Yoon, 2001). Collaborative professional development frees teachers' minds to "do the kind of powerful, professional, critical thinking that moves [their teaching and their students] forward" (Pardini, 2004).

Through collaboration, the teacher encounters multiple perspectives, which challenge pre-existing knowledge and beliefs. This in turn, promotes reflection as the teacher negotiates meaning from these different perspectives. Thus, framing teacher learning in collaborative environments empowers teachers to "reflect on their own interpretations, construct alternative meanings and expand their perspective" (Fung, 2000, p. 156).

Highly collaborative schools view professional development as an ongoing process rather than an event on a single day. These schools are continuously reviewing, analyzing, and most importantly, discussing student work and ongoing curricular needs to discern patterns and make adjustments. Collaboration is undertaken in a spirit of collegiality with respect and interdependence among all involved. It is important that library media specialists participate in these discussions as often as possible so that they can be aware of needs and concerns in their school community. Further, when presenting professional development, the library media specialists must recognize that simply "telling" colleagues may inform them, but does not allow them to develop any form of meaningful understanding, much less to grasp how to integrate new information into their practice. Giving teachers time for discussion is essential to creating disequilibrium that confronts old beliefs and enables the assimilation of new information.

Reflective Practice

Yet another flaw in traditional professional development is found in the time constraints of traditional workshops, combined with lecturer-centered modes of delivery. This lethal combination limits opportunities for teachers to engage in reflection. Trainers using this model assume that simply telling educators what they need to know will generate automatic acceptance and educators will integrate new information into their practice without question. Reflective practice, characterized as carefully examining one's own and others' practices in order to strengthen the quality and the effectiveness of their work, is associated with changes in teacher practice and improvements in student achievement (Sparks & Loucks-Horsley, 1989). John Dewey (1938/1997) acknowledged the necessity for reflection and differentiated between routine action and reflective action in teachers. Reflection enables teachers to consider their practice and act in a deliberate and intentional fashion rather than simply act in a blind and impulsive manner.

Powerful professional development for library media specialists recognizes that reflection is important in creating and sustaining change. Library media specialists must be given opportunities to think critically and to make meaning of their professional development experience. Rather than simply accept new strategies at face value, they must have time and opportunities to consider readings, discuss with colleagues, to journal, or to participate in mentoring relationships. This process allows library media specialists to examine long-held beliefs that underlie practice and to gain insight into the assumptions that sustain these beliefs. Rethinking old attitudes and beliefs allows library media specialists to become consciously aware of how these existing networks of belief influence practice and how change may yield benefits to students and faculty. This process is not instantaneous and requires time beyond a single in-service event. Further, successful library media specialists do not limit reflection just to professional development but engage in ongoing reflection about their practice.

Similarly, professional development by library media specialists should also incorporate opportunities for reflection. Teachers, just like library media specialists, develop patterns of practice based on deeply embedded assumptions about learning. New concepts or strategies will not necessarily meet with instant acceptance and must be challenged through structured opportunities for reflection. Reflection exposes old assumptions to the light of new understandings of learning and can initiate the process of change.

Active Learning

Many older library media specialists have memories of being crowded into hot auditoriums with teachers from a dozen other schools to hear a "renowned" speaker lecture for an entire day on a "topic of interest" that only vaguely related to the situation at their school. If they stole a glance at their colleagues, they might see them balancing their checkbook, grading papers, or even nodding off. This type of professional development views teachers as passive receivers of information. Rather than actively engaging in construction of knowledge, teachers in this scenario are expected to simply absorb knowledge from an expert and to replicate its content or methodology in their school.

Effective professional development provides opportunities for active and participatory learning experiences. Giving educators opportunities to be actively engaged in constructing professional knowledge is viewed as essential to improving their knowledge, understanding, and ability. Active learning activities may include discussion, role-play, debate, curriculum writing, working with a new technology, and so forth. Active participation in their professional development allows educators to take part in the same kind of learning experiences that they should be providing to their students. Whether the professional development content focuses on new pedagogies, new technologies or greater understanding of the content in the domain, hands-on learning will enhance the quality of learning within professional development. Ultimately, active participation creates learner-centered environments and shifts the responsibility for learning from the professional development facilitator to the participant.

Whether active learning should be included in professional development both for and by library media specialists is no longer the issue. Instead, the focus should be on evaluating professional development plans to determine where "hands-on" learning activities may be included. Simply telling participants about new research strategies or new technologies will not result in the same depth of learning as those that encourage active learning. The most frequently cited reason for neglecting active learning is a lack of time for these types of activities. However, the power of active learning is too great to be ignored. Plans should be evaluated allowing active learning to assume priority over other objectives.

Providing Follow-Up Support

Finally, the one-day workshop approach to professional development prevalent in most school districts does not address the need for continuing support in the implementation of in-service themes and content. While teachers are left with handouts and notes at the end of a workshop, there is typically little follow-up support to ensure that they implement new programs properly or that their concerns are adequately addressed (Joyce & Showers, 1988). If follow-up is neglected, only 5 percent to 10 percent of educators attending a workshop will implement the strategies presented.

The ultimate goal for teacher professional development is educator learning that promotes changes in the educator's knowledge, understanding, behaviors, skills, values, and beliefs (Hord, 1994). Without continuing assistance and support, variously referred to as *follow-up, sustained involvement,* or *follow-through,* the traditional model of professional development overrates the teacher's capacity for change (Fullan, 1991). Through follow-up, educators are afforded the time to participate in discussions that enhance understanding,

Professional Development Format

Mention professional development, however, and most educators instantly envision the workshop model, a model where educators are released from their school responsibilities to attend workshops. Workshops vary in duration from a couple of hours to the whole day. They may be offered at the school or district or at associated educational institutions. The underlying assumption of this model is that professional development is a discrete event set apart from the daily routine and, in some cases, from the campus. Unfortunately, this model has become the dominant method of professional development in American education.

Successful professional learning is viewed as ongoing and builds upon previous knowledge and experience. An alternative view of professional development recognizes that professional learning should be ongoing and embedded in school practice rather than a one-time event. This view acknowledges that change is not instantaneous and supports the educators' need to consider, discuss, and reflect on innovations over time.

The following professional development formats are gaining support in American education and meet the criteria for effective professional development. These formats may be used to extend learning from workshops, in combination with each other, or even as a stand-alone. Schools that engage in these types of job-embedded professional development formats become professional learning communities.

- ***Action Research:*** *The focus in action research is on examining real issues or problems in the school environment and using problem solving techniques to seek resolution. Educators identify questions for research derived from their practice, collect data, analyze and interpret the data, and apply their findings to their own practice.*

- ***Curriculum Writing:*** *Through writing curriculum, educators are immersed in both the content and the pedagogy of a discipline. Typically, this approach begins with grounding educators in the discipline content and may branch into the underlying learning theories and pedagogical models that support student learning. As teachers become engaged in the process, they take ownership of the final product and are more likely to use the lessons they have developed. Content standards guide the instructional design process.*

- ***Demonstrations:*** *The oft-quoted statement that "Seeing is believing" can apply to the implementation phase of new innovations in schools. Educators may need to see a new strategy demonstrated in order to be able to implement it with fidelity. Many large districts have curriculum or technology specialists who are available to present demonstration lessons in the school. Viewing video demonstrations also allows teachers to see new strategies in practice, but with the additional benefit of being able to stop and review the video. One variant of this format originating in Japan is the Lesson Study where teams of teachers (grade level, department.) prepare a lesson that is demonstrated in a classroom for other teachers and invited guests. At the conclusion of the lesson, a debriefing session is held where observers ask questions. The team is accountable for the success or failure of the lesson.*

- ***Mentoring:*** *Professional development in the form of mentoring programs can have a significant impact in supporting novices. Mentoring programs have been implemented for a variety of novices, beginning educators, educators beginning new assignments, or educators learning to integrate technology into their practice. Although it is generally accepted that the mentee benefits from the relationship, the mentor also benefits through the process of sharing skills and knowledge gained through extensive professional practice*

- ***Peer Coaching:*** *This format enables educators to learn from each other through collegial observations and feedback about classroom performance. Peer coaching depends on an atmosphere of trust, respect, and a willingness to change. Several steps are necessary for the success of this format. Prior to observation, colleagues agree on the criteria to be observed. During observation, anecdotal notes are taken. Following observation, discussions are held to review what was noted.*

- ***Study Group:*** *Through small group meetings, educators deepen their knowledge about a topic. These meetings may focus on extending knowledge in a content domain, book study, or student needs. Through regular meetings, educators develop a community of learning centered on the study group topic.*

Regardless of whether the campus adopts the workshop format or one of the alternative formats, opportunities for leadership by library media specialists abound. These opportunities may be viewed through the lens of leadership roles of the library media specialist. Lance (n.d.) has identified five roles common to the work of library media specialists who impact student achievement: school leader, program administrator, information navigator, technology facilitator, and collaborative teacher and learner. The interaction of the various roles and professional development experiences can lead to powerful change in schools.

As a school leader, the library media specialist should be a member of those committees and institutions that contribute to school effectiveness. As a member of the campus leadership team, for example, the library media specialist can participate in examinations of student data and help chart the course that the campus takes regarding professional development. Engaging in planning for professional development reinforces the importance of the school library as a viable partner in preparing students for academic success.

As a program administrator, the library media specialist is responsible for managing all activities related to the library program including budgeting, staffing, scheduling, collection development both print and electronic, promotion, instruction, and outreach to the public library/community. As the professional development program evolves in a school, the library media specialist must take a critical look at these activities and determine how the library can support the needs of the school community. If, for example, a high school is focusing on improving science achievement, the library media specialist should meet with the science department chair to gain a greater understanding of the direction that that science instruction will take. By attending science department meetings, the library media specialist can get input from the science department on ways that the library can support the instructional changes that are in the offing. It may mean looking at the science collection to determine weaknesses, examining policies to determine how to promote equitable access to the library and its materials, and looking for resources within the community to support science understanding. Throughout the process, the library media specialist should regularly promote the role that the library is taking to support science success to the school community and its stakeholders.

As an information navigator, the library media specialist can serve as a resource expert. Every year a myriad of educational books and articles rise to the publishing surface, clamoring for attention in the public arena. Through his or her own professional development, the library media specialist develops rich understandings of new learning theories, emerging pedagogies and practices, or technology integration strategies. Thus, the library media specialist can filter the choices and supply relevant information to teacher learners. A campus study group, for example, may need assistance in choosing appropriate materials for their topic. The library media specialist can then recommend relevant books and articles for study groups that focus on their chosen topics. As a technology facilitator, the library media specialist can mentor faculty and connect teachers' fragmented knowledge of educational technology with his or her own rich knowledge of information literacy. Through an ongoing process of mentoring, the library media specialist can enhance teachers' technology tools, understandings of databases, ethical uses of information, and the integrity of information on the Internet. Mentoring teachers on educational technology can take place through planning collaborative lessons, providing brochures and fliers to teachers connecting database resources to curriculum, or participating on technology committees. Fulfilling this role of mentor sustains the vision of the school library as an information technology hub and the librarian as a technology leader in education.

As a collaborative teacher and learner, Lance (n.d.) notes that the librarian is both a teacher of students and a teacher of teachers. Oftentimes, working with students in the library is uncharted territory for a teacher. Although we hold the expectation that teachers will come to us for collaboration on student research in the library, we can encounter resistance from teachers who lack a mental model for the capacity of their students or the design of the experience. Reaching beyond the library doors, library media specialists can scaffold their understanding by taking on a greater share of the initial responsibility. This may mean designing and teaching demonstration lessons with their students, either in the classroom or in the library. Working with teachers in this capacity establishes the library media specialist as an instructional peer with a unique knowledge framework that advances the school's academic vision and goals. As teachers participate in successful experiences in the library, they build understandings of the instructional design and the value of this type of instruction creating the opportunity for future collaborations.

Evaluation

Evaluation of professional development experiences is an often-neglected process viewed by educators as a waste of time (Guskey, 2000). If an evaluation is conducted at all, it is typically a superficial process that focuses on the "happiness quotient" of the experience (Sparks, 1997). Questions in this type of evaluation have measured participants' satisfaction with issues that range from the warmth of the room to the enjoyment of the refreshments to the comfort of the chairs. High marks in this type of evaluation may indeed reflect satisfaction with the experience, but have little to do with how this experience promotes and sustains educator growth.

Guskey (2000) favors a more systematic approach to evaluating professional development and suggests a comprehensive five-level analysis of professional development programs distributed over time. The levels progress from simple to complex with each level supporting the next. Successful implementation at one level depends on successful implementation of the prior level. These levels include Participants' Reactions, Participants' Learning, Response of Organizational Culture, Participants' Use of New Skills, and Student Outcomes.

Participants' Reactions

Guskey does not dispute the necessity for surveying participants' for their reactions to professional development as long as it is part of a multilevel analysis. It is important to understand whether participants' felt their human needs were addressed, whether they "liked" the experience, and whether the content made sense to them. This information can be used as a formative evaluation for facilitators either validating the design or helping them to identify trouble spots and make adjustments to their programs (Champion, 2003). Typically a short survey gathers this information.

Participants' Learning

Traditionally, successful completion of professional development meant completing the "hours" required for professional development. The second level in Guskey's model determines whether participants' have gained the knowledge, skills, or attitudes that were the intended outcomes of the professional development program. This may be addressed through paper and pencil quizzes, journals, skill demonstrations, and course products. At the outset, participants' should be alerted to the criteria and indicators for successful learning that will be required at the conclusion.

Organizational Culture

The norms and culture of each school deeply influence the outcomes of professional development leading to the third level of the evaluation, organizational support, and change. This level assesses the impact of the new program or innovation on the organizational culture of the school. This analysis tries to answer questions such as:

- How do organizational policies of the district or school support the new program or innovation?
- Are problems with the program or innovation being addressed?
- Are appropriate resources being allocated to support the innovation?

This level of the evaluation is not addressed initially and is intentionally delayed to give time for participants' to begin implementation. Guskey recommends information to evaluate this level can be obtained from direct observations, minutes from meetings, document reviews, questionnaires, or interviews.

Use of New Skills

At the fourth level, the focus is on participants' use of new knowledge and skills. This level attempts to discern to what degree and with what fidelity are new skills being integrated into practice. Assessment of participants' use of new knowledge and skills is not done immediately to allow participants' time to adopt new ideas and begin using them. Rather, assessments are made at regular intervals over a span of several months. Direct observations, interviews, portfolios, and personal reflections can be used for the evaluation at this level.

Student Outcomes

The final level examines the impact of professional development on student learning. The focus of this analysis is to determine whether the professional development program has had an impact on student outcomes in academic, behavioral, or other areas. Indicators could be standardized tests, grades, discipline referrals, homework completion, or attitudinal surveys.

Although the process of evaluation may be tedious and time consuming, the information it yields will provide valuable information as to the success of the professional development program and ultimately how it impacts student outcomes. See Figure 7.1.

Figure 7.1 Guskey's Model

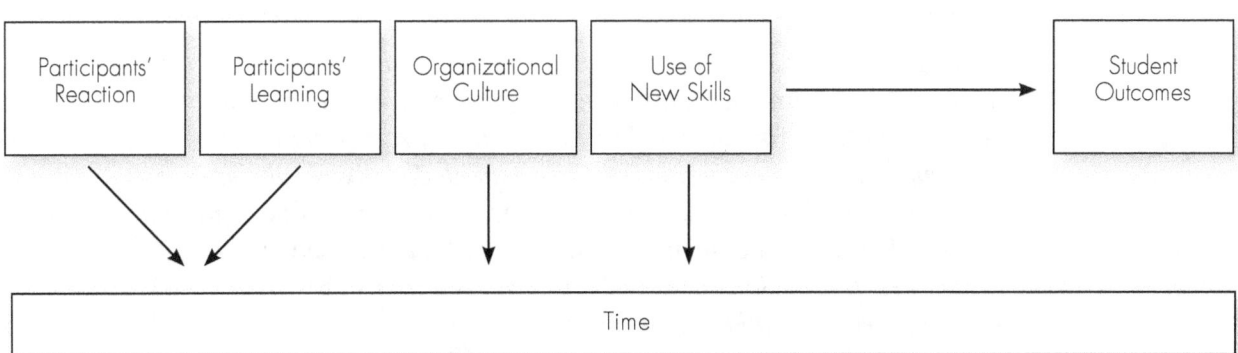

Tips for Planning an Effective Professional Development Program

Professional development is not simply creating a PowerPoint presentation with all the whiz-bang transitions and clever transformations. Powerful professional development begins in the planning stages and incorporates the concepts and ideals that have been discussed in this chapter. The following eight questions provide a framework for creating a professional development program. Although they are listed in numerical order, many of the questions are intertwined and decisions will be made concurrently.

1) *What are the needs for professional development?*

Planning for professional development should begin with the end goals for student learning or behavior in mind (Guskey, 2001). As you begin planning for professional development, consider where student performance is lacking. What types of professional development would enable students to be more successful?

2) *How do needs align with district goals, content standards, performance standards?*

This question is intertwined with question one. Obviously, there can be many needs, but those needs that enable institutional goals or help meet state standards or benchmarks should receive priority. When considering topics for professional development, library media specialists will need to consider how these topics help students meet these goals and standards. Rather than simply presenting a database as a new resource, library media specialists should also present its relationship to state curriculum frameworks and how it enables student performance on those frameworks.

3) *Content to be included?*

As with planning any lesson, begin by specifying the learning objectives that teacher-learners will be able to do upon successful completion of the professional development. Consider what prior knowledge is required. Determine what content can be included in the time frame for the professional development.

4) *Format to be used?*

Although there are a variety of formats for professional development, determine which one best fits the needs of your content and faculty. Consider a library media specialist planning a professional development program on rubrics. If an extended study of rubrics is necessary, the library media specialist should consider a study group. On the other hand, faculty may be writing new curriculum where rubrics are appropriate, and incorporating it into the curriculum writing process would be appropriate.

5) *Incorporation of best practices?*

Look back over the discussion of best practices included earlier in the chapter. How will the activities included in the professional development program enable collaboration among participants? Reflection? Active Learning? How will follow-up support be provided?

6) **Evaluation of professional development?**

Create a plan for evaluation that includes as many of the five levels of Guskey's plan as possible. Create a tickler file that would remind you to check back on professional development at regular intervals to determine how well teachers are using new skills.

[7] **What resources will be needed?**

Determine what resources would be needed for the professional development program. If an action research group, for example, chooses to study student reading performance, determine what resources the library can provide either through circulation reports or Accelerated Reader reports. If a new history database is being presented, will computers be available for every participant to facilitate active exploration of the database?

[8] **What budgetary funds will be needed?**

Create a budget for the professional development program. What are the costs for materials? What are the costs for refreshments? Where will the funds for these costs be found?

Look for Opportunities

Many library media specialists secretly wish that they could be part of the professional development program at their school. Often, however, faculty meetings and in-service days are filled by district and governmental mandates leaving very little time for professional development related to library and information literacy. This does not mean that professional development from the library media specialist is not needed or wanted. The library media specialist has a rich background in information literacy that supports the success of the students and faculty. Providing professional development for faculty is both an expectation and a responsibility.

Look for opportunities. Start by looking over the list of alternative forms of professional development for a possible format that could be delivered outside of in-service days. Consider offering your own workshops before or after school. Pair with a teacher colleague and prepare a presentation.

If necessary, start with a simple project. Create a handout about topics such as how to access the library catalog from the classroom. Share a new technology at a department or grade level meeting. Place a list of resources for an upcoming unit in a teacher's box.

Summary

No matter what the level of the library media specialist's involvement is in providing professional development, this visibility validates the library media specialist's leadership role in the school. The library media specialist constantly seeks to enhance her own knowledge and skills so that she may serve as an instructional leader on the campus. However, the school library does not exist in a vacuum, but is dependent on frequent, constant interactions with the school community. Collaborative partnerships with stakeholders in the school community ensure that professional development is both consistent with the school's vision and relevant to the participants. Working with faculty, the library media specialist determines needs for professional development and works to find opportunities to build staff knowledge about information literacies. Incorporating best practices and developing a plan for evaluation helps to sustain use of knowledge and skills gained in the professional development program.

Works Cited

Champion, R. (2003). Taking measure: The real measure of a professional development program's effectiveness lies in what participants learn. *Journal of Staff Development*, (24), 75-76.

Darling-Hammond, L. (1998). Teacher learning that supports student learning. *Educational Leadership*, 55 (5), 6-11.

Dewey, J. (1938/1997). *Experience and education*. New York: Simon and Schuster.

Fullan, M. with Stiegelbauer, S. (1991). *The new meaning of educational change (2nd ed.)*. New York: Teachers College Press.

Fung, Y. (2000). A constructivist strategy for developing teachers for change. *Journal of In-service Education, 26(1)*, 153-167.

Garet, M. S., Porter, A. C., Desimone, L., Birman, B. F., & Yoon, K. S. (2001, Winter). What makes professional development effective? Results from a national sample of teachers. *American Educational Research Journal*, 38(4), 915-945.

Goodlad, J. I. (1984). *A place called school: Prospects for the future*. New York: McGraw-Hill.

Guskey, T. R. (2000). *Evaluating professional development*. Thousand Oaks, CA: Corwin Press.

Guskey, T. R. (2001, Summer). The backward approach. *Journal of Staff Development*, 22(3), 60.

Hamilton-Pennell, C., Lance, K. C., Rodney, M. J., & Hainer, E. (2000). Dick and Jane go to the head of the class. *School Library Journal*, 46(4), 44-47.

Hord, S. M. (1994). Staff development and change process: Cut from the same cloth. *Issues . . . about Change, 4(2)*, 1-6.

Joyce, B., & Showers, B. (1988). *Student achievement through staff development*. White Plains, NY: Longman Press.

Kaiser Family Foundation. New study finds children aged zero to six spend as much time with TV, computers and video games as playing outside. 28 Oct 2003. Henry J. Kaiser Family Foundation. 17 Jun 2005. http://www.kff.org/entmedia/entmedia102903nr.cfm.

Lance, K. C. (n.d.). *5 roles for empowering library media specialists*. LibraryResearch Service Colorado State Library. Retrieved March 15, 2005 from http://www.lrs.org/documents/lmcstudies/5roles.pdf

Little, J. W. (1992). Opening the black box of professional community. In A. Lieberman (Ed.), *The changing contexts of teaching* (158–178). Chicago: University of Chicago Press.

Loucks-Horsley, S., Harding, C. K., Arbuckle, M. A., Murray, L. B., Dubea, C., & Williams, M. K. (1987). *Continuing to learn: A guidebook for teacher development*. Andover, MA: Regional Laboratory for Educational Improvement of the Northeast & Islands.

National Education Commission on Time and Learning [NECTL]. (1994). Prisoners of time. Washington, DC: Author. ED366115 [Available on-line: gopher://gopher.ed.gov:70/00/ publications/full[underscore]text/PoTResearch/5; http://www.ed.gov/pubs/PrisonersOfTime/index.html]

Pardini, P. (2004, Winter). Valley cultivates comprehensive process. *Journal of Staff Development, 25(1)*, 42-45.

Schunk, D. (2000). *Learning theories: An educational perspective*. Columbus, OH: Merrill Publishing Co.

Shroyer, M. G. (1990). Effective staff development for effective organization development. *Journal of Staff Development, 11(1)*, 2-6.

Smylie, M. A., & Conyers, J. G. (1991, Winter). Changing conceptions of teaching influence the future of staff development. *Journal of Staff Development, 12(1)*, 12-16.

Sparks, D., & Hirsch, S. (1997). *A new vision for staff development*. Oxford, OH: National Staff Development Council.

Sparks, D., & Loucks-Horsley, S. (1989, Fall). Five models of staff development for teachers. *Journal of Staff Development, 10(4)*, 40-57.

CHAPTER EIGHT:
LEARNER-CENTERED TEACHING: Information Access and Leadership

Barbara Bertoldo

In times past, *literacy* focused on the ability to read and write. In the present we are in the center of an ongoing information revolution that necessitates evolution of the term literacy and its meaning into something far more complex. *Literacy* now encompasses a broad spectrum of meanings couched in information and all its forms. The North Central Regional Educational Laboratory Web site, NCREL (2004), identifies digital-age literacy to include the following:

- *basic literacy,*
- *scientific literacy,*
- *economic literacy,*
- *technological literacy,*
- *visual literacy,*
- *information literacy,*
- *multicultural literacy, and*
- *global awareness literacy.*

It is no wonder that school libraries struggle to meet the literacy needs of their students and staff as well as the demands of new and emerging technologies. The need for information literacy instruction requires a change in the way we, as teacher-librarians, prepare information and teach. It not only requires reform *but* commitment to reform. For literacy to be effectively taught and student achievement enhanced, everyone in the school must become involved in the teaching process; thus, the school becomes "learner-centered." It only stands to reason, then, that librarians are the leaders in the 21st century digital-age literacy movement. Tony Wagner (1998) states that, "Although other educators acknowledge the importance of information literacy instruction, librarians are the first to develop standards and indicators for information literacy goals and objectives" (p. 5, 13).

What then should school administrators, teachers, students, and community members expect from their school libraries in this new age? Twenty-first-century school libraries should strive to become learner-centered. Once a learner-centered framework is built, collaboration as well as good teaching and engaged learning become the norm. The components of a learner-centered environment condense to six basic standards that every library can adopt:

- *learner-centered teaching and learning,*
- *learner-centered program leadership and management,*
- *learner-centered technology and information access,*
- *learner-centered library environment,*
- *learner-centered connections to community, and*
- *learner-centered librarianship.*

How does the library develop a plan for successful change once learner-centered standards have been established? What essential elements should a library media center incorporate to meet challenges presented by the digital age and ensure that students and staff are successful users of ideas and information? *The Information Power* logo illustrates Information Literacy Standards for Student Learning encircled by Collaboration, Leadership, and Technology, then three intersecting circles that represent Learning and Teaching, Information Access and Delivery, and Program Administration (AASL & AECT, 1998, p. 48). How do these elements translate to a real school setting? How can these elements be incorporated into a library media center program that strives to maintain a balance between the essential elements and creating student achievement within a learner-centered environment?

This chapter covers fundamental recommendations for creating such a program and the leadership role required for each.

The Librarian as Teacher

The librarian as teacher knows the curriculum in general terms, collaborates, and communicates with teachers to assist in achieving learner-centered goals that align with state curriculum standards.

Educators now face the challenge of providing state and national standards-based instruction. Many feel that standards-based instruction is restrictive and binding, and to some degree it is. Standards-driven teaching can expose deficiencies in the teaching process as well as the curriculum, but the process can be undermined if teachers feel that they lose flexibility when planning and presenting lessons that are tied to standards. The rigidity becomes more pronounced as they struggle to find innovative ways to present what appears to them as a standards-bound curriculum rather than a standards-based curriculum.

In a standards-based learning environment the curriculum is focused on learner-centered activities. Carol Kuhlthau notes in *Information Power* (1998), "When not guided in the use of a process, students tend to approach research as though there is only one right answer, and fail to learn how to use information to construct their own meaning" (p. 5).

Research also indicates that when schools that focus their energy on techniques develop information literacy skills anchored in a standards-based, information-rich environment, they see greater success in student achievement. Such improved performance is a natural consequence of the transformation from passive learners to engaged, active learners surrounded by standards-based lessons.

Case Study A

In a present-day high school, the librarians typically work with faculty to design units that align with state-adopted textbooks. For AP Biology classes studying DNA and RNA, the librarian and the teacher collaboratively design an interactive DNA Web page that includes use of technology, team-teaching, and alignment to a state standards-based curriculum that allows for student outcomes and achievement. To establish and encourage the use of critical thinking skills, the librarian asks students to identify three basic questions before starting their research:

- *What do I already know about this topic?*
- *What more do I need to know?*
- *What is the main question I want to answer?*

Working from an interactive Web page that incorporates media clips into the guided instruction, students gather information, answer teacher-developed questions, and participate in an online quiz. Students capitalize on their natural ability to weave together images, text, and sound to learn at their own pace as well as work collaboratively in groups; however, they must still be guided by the team (the teacher and the librarian) while they use the interactive Web page that has been constructed, by the library staff, for this specific exercise. This process of working has been identified as bricolage—"the ability to piece informational strands together and make coherent sense of them" (Scribner, 2004). Marc Prensky (2005) writes in his article, "Digital Natives, Digital Immigrants, Part II: Do They Really Think Differently," that today's youth, the NextGens, think outside traditional parameters; "They develop hypertext minds; they leap around" (n.p.). Another important aspect to remember when working with today's student is the constant need for subtle guidance as they work in collaborative environments. Because these tech-savvy, communication-centric students know how to use technology intimately, and they have the ability to multitask as part of their core being, educators often make the mistake of thinking that this millennial generation's inherent tech-abilities allow them to work easily in an information-rich environment without guidance, that they inherently know how to conduct a relevant search or understand how to adequately evaluate information once they have located it.

Furthermore, today's students are resistant to formal instruction if it does not meet the litmus test of being easy to use and streamlined. Educators all too often make the mistake of thinking that a student who is working quietly at a computer is accessing the right resources. However, research has proven that students need subtle guidance, and that they need to pay attention to the ongoing learning activity, and attach meaning to the activity. In essence, they need purpose to learn (Ediger, 2004). In this kind of constructivist learning environment, the teacher and librarian become guides to help students answer the three basic questions listed above.

The Librarian as Innovator and Collaborator

The librarian as innovator and collaborator attends curriculum workshops.

Case Study B

Active participation in workshop sessions can do much to foster collaboration between teachers and the librarian. For example, a progressive, leadership-oriented librarian finds opportunities to connect with teachers on their terms. In this case study, the librarian attends a full-day workshop designed to prepare third grade teachers for new initiatives in reading instruction. Approximately 150 third-grade teachers and this single teacher-librarian have assembled to learn from district reading specialists about new initiatives in reading instruction. Several times during the presentation, the librarian is able to illustrate how the library can support the new reading initiatives with resources and lesson plans that encourage direct integration of information literacy skills and technology into the teacher's curriculum. Not only does this library professional's participation persuade teachers from his school to see him as one of the team, other participants will go back to their schools eager to seek the expertise of their own school librarian.

The Librarian as Part of the Administrative Team

The librarian as part of the administrative team is aware of and supports the school's learning and teaching goals and objectives.

Case Study C

At elementary schools where a librarian has taken on the leadership role of teaching and learning, grade-level teams plan units of instruction for each subject. These units may be as simple as brief planning calendars for the entire year. The librarian makes a point of gathering copies of each plan as they are devised. Based on the collected unit plans, the librarian is able to schedule and support teachers' efforts for each grade-level and partner with the teacher to work with individual grades on projects each semester. In this way, the majority of the cross-curricular units, collaboratively planned, will integrate information literacy and technology as they are executed in both the library and the classroom while meeting the campus plan's teaching and learning goals and objectives.

The Librarian as a Leader, Listening, Identifying, Creating Opportunities

Always and enthusiastically, librarians take advantage of every chance to assist a teacher with support materials, ideas, and professional resources.

Case Study D

To illustrate this point, a library professional who is leadership-oriented will work with the school's administrators to schedule faculty departmental meetings in the library promoting, demonstrating, and facilitating the use of new or previously underused resources directly applicable to members of each specific department. This kind of informal professional development should be ongoing throughout the year. Working with the administration, the library may request that these sessions become part of the technology proficiency requirements for the school or district. They may even expand on the idea of giving teachers continuing education hours as part of the incentive for attendance. It becomes imperative that the teacher-librarian is aware of the capabilities of their faculty members. Once the more reluctant technology users, usually the older teachers, agree to commit themselves to the technology-stretch, every effort should be made to assist them in the steep learning curve. The same tenets of teaching and learning that guide our student-based instruction should also guide our professional development instruction, as shown in Figure 8.1.

Figure 8.1 Professional Development Checklist

Professional Development Checklist

- *Demonstrate genuine understanding of each faculty member's abilities.*
- *Develop presentations with concrete sequential elements that focus on skills that develop information literacy skills. The University of Texas-Austin Digital Library has developed an excellent online prototype called TILT specifically used for the development of information literacy skills with both students and teachers.*
- *Facilitate faculty learning by organizing materials with plenty of hands-on exercises.*
- *Develop a process for remediation (one-on-one sessions, tutorials, guides, and exercises) for those who may be having difficulty until they gain confidence with the process.*
- *Develop collegial professional environments by relating our user's needs to the services we as teacher-librarians can provide.*

The Learner-Centered Professional Development schematic, shown in Figure 8.2 gives a visual for the kind of learning environment libraries should establish to assist faculty with their technology proficiency.

Figure 8.1   *Learner-centered Professional Development Schematic*

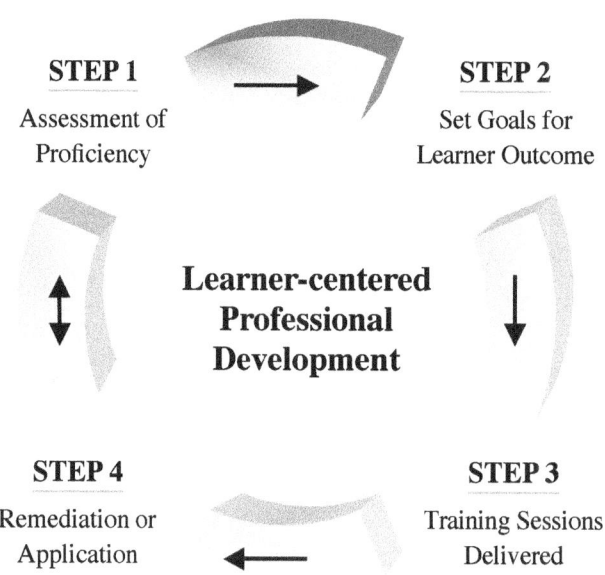

When librarians add to the arsenal of tools available to the classroom teacher, the quality of instruction improves and the librarian will soon be included in more instructional planning while promoting the library program as effective and engaging. Last but not least, be service-oriented! Anticipate the user's needs!

Information Access & Literacy

The librarian as leader stays abreast of education trends and developments. Younger students access the library print collection to develop their own reading rhythms; older students access the library print and electronic collections more to fill their information needs and less for their recreational reading needs. The OCLC 2004 Information Format Trends Report indicates that reading/literacy skills may be diminished because students spend less time reading than using technology. The Kaiser Foundation reports on average that students use multimedia two hours per day compared to 22 minutes of reading per day. The Pew Institute reports, "seventy-three percent of students needing information are more likely to use the Internet instead of the library for their research" (n.p.). This same report also states:

> *Internet-savvy students rely on the Internet to help them do their schoolwork. They describe dozens of different education-related uses of the Internet. Virtually all use the Internet to do research to help them write papers or complete class work or homework assignments. Generally students employ five different metaphors to explain how they use the Internet for school: The Internet as virtual textbook and reference library, as virtual tutor and study shortcut, as virtual study group, as virtual guidance counselor, and the Internet as virtual locker, backpack, and notebook (n.p.).*

Case Study E

This case study will give insight into the way students may use familiar technologies to complete a classroom assignment.

A second grade class is doing research in the library on a mammal or bird that they would like to learn more about. Their teacher tells each student that he may present the information in any format, but all reports must answer a series of questions:

1) What is the name of your animal or bird?

2) Where does your animal or bird live?

3) What does your animal or bird eat?

4) What color is your animal or bird?

5) How large does your animal or bird grow?

6) Tell one interesting fact about your animal or bird.

Students complete their research both in the library and in the classroom, presenting their final projects. Many of the projects are displayed on poster board. Some students have made puppets; others simply write a report and draw pictures. However, two children have found a unique way to present their information.

Child 1: This child's father is a local television news anchorman. The animal chosen is the grizzly bear. This young second grader has decided to produce a taped interview using his large teddy bear while he, dressed in suit and tie, acts as the television news anchorman with his father taping the interview. During the interview the bear is too shy to speak to the camera and will only whisper his answers to the anchorman. However, each of the six questions is asked of the bear, and the answers for all six are given in return to fulfill the criteria for the assignment. Clearly, this young child has utilized technology to his advantage, capturing the attention of everyone and confidently presenting all the information required of him.

Child 2: Another student from this same second grade class has decided to research a barn swallow because he has been watching a pair of swallows construct a nest under the eave of his family home. He has decided to take pictures of the barn swallow's activity, but the family is leaving for vacation before the eggs hatch. The student's father suggests that they use the family's digital camera's time-lapsed feature and capture the hatching of the eggs as they emerge into young chicks over the 10-day period. The camera is set on time-lapse mode while the family is on vacation. The final project is presented as a series of digital images morphed (using the software photo manager that the father uses for his job) into a continuous time sequence to show the hatching and growth of the chicks. The young student is taught how to manipulate the software program to complete his assignment. He has already finished the research part of the project, answering the six questions that satisfy the criteria for the report. The final project holds the attention of his class and teachers as he tells the story of the young hatchlings using digital images. At the end of his presentation, a click of the mouse sends the images into a morph, and the hatching process builds magically to its climax of young, squawking barn swallow chicks.

Clearly, both of these children had unique methods for presenting their information. As a result of their interests and use of technology, they learned through discovery, becoming thoroughly engaged in the learning process.

As students progress through the secondary grades, their learning characteristics become more pronounced. We find that the characteristics of 21st-century high school students, a group sometimes called "Millenials, NetGens, or Generation Ys," have been described by some as *format agnostics, experiential, and adaptive.* Research indicates that this generation will impact libraries in ways that have not been imagined. A comparison of the learning characteristics and use of technology of NetGens (1985-present) and that of the WW I & II Generation (1918-1948), Baby Boomers (1949-1968), the Echo Boomers or Generation Xers (1969-1985) shows attributes that work well in an Internet-driven society. See Figure 8.3 below.

Figure 8.3 Generational Learning Characteristics

Generational Learning Characteristics

WW I & II Generation (1918-1948)	Baby Boomers (1949-1968)	Generation X, Echo Boomers (1969-1985)	Generation Y, NetGens (1985-present)
• Respects authority • Patriotic • Civically involved • Schedule-oriented • Reluctant to use technology • Technologies geared to ease industrial work • Radio used for information and entertainment • Silent movies as form of entertainment in metropolitan areas • Reading books and newspapers for pleasure and information	• Flower children questioning authority (teens & 20s) • Workaholics (30s, 40s, 50s) • First generation college grads • More time for entertainment as music industry explodes with 78rpm records and HiFis • Technologies accelerated due to the Space Race (Advent of artificial intelligence and smart machines) • Black & white television • Movies with sound • Early children's programming in black & white • Explosion of the music industry • Newspapers, nightly news, and radio still main avenue for news	• Skeptical of Baby Boomer parents' work ethic • Attempts to create balance between work and play • Job-sharing in vogue • Resistive to collaborative efforts • Loners • Early multitaskers • Technologies: Home computers used for games and some word processing • Advent of boom box, VCRs, and color television in every home • Television watching increases as children's programming grows • Advent of headline news programming allows viewer to get news anytime without reading a newspaper • Web emerges, strives to build content not context • Reading for pleasure declines	• Enjoys collaborative learning and working on teams • Multitaskers • Graphic/digital image acuity from image-rich environment • Refuse to read large amounts of text • Easily bored if not interested in subject • Highly competitive academically and technically • Technologically-centric • Technologies: MP3s, digital cameras, cell phones, wireless computing, PDAs, instant messaging • Movies produced with digital enhancements and can download to a cell phone • Personal DVD players • Information can be obtained virtually from any electronic information source 24/7 • News can be downloaded from any source • Reading literacy skills in a downward spiral • Library day is every day 24/7

On July 31, 2002, the Washington Post reported, "To be young is to be cognitively welded to a mobile" (C1). Likewise, OCLC reports in their 2004 Information Format Trends Report that in 2002, 31 billion e-mails traveled the Web on a daily basis. By 2006, that number is predicted to double to 60 billion per day. OCLC in their Trends format report predicts the shift in other kinds of Web content by year 2009.

Interestingly enough, the NetGen students of today will become the educators of tomorrow, and as such, they will use technology and their unique tech-savvy on a level never before seen (Oblinger, 2005).

The librarian as facilitator provides access to classes in an inviting, welcoming climate and remembers that the library belongs to the learning community. The library exists to support student literacy, learning, and instruction by the teaching staff and must be perceived as open and committed to this objective. Teachers may schedule a weekly or bi-weekly time to bring the entire class for checking out books. These scheduled check-out times require a library assistant managing the circulation desk. The librarian's focus should be furthering the educational objectives of the school. Circulation of materials does not necessarily require the librarian's presence.

Even though the library is busy with various activities simultaneously underway, an atmosphere for learning and thinking must be maintained. Many times, the library's physical facility is another disconnect for today's student. Libraries of the past were characteristically quiet, providing sparse, uncomfortable seating that was conducive only to formal individual study. After guidance from insightful library leaders, many architects designing new school libraries are now designing common areas within the library itself. The reason is simply to address the learning styles of today's students. Recalling the attributes of 21st-century learner, we know that they are social, that they think in multi-dimensions, and that they have grown up in a relaxed atmosphere where many different activities are happening simultaneously (O'Reilly, 2000, p. 154).

The leadership role where facilities are concerned enlists outside assistance from Friends of the Library, groups, parents, and community members. In this arena, the librarian capitalizes on the idea that the library environment belongs not only to students, but also to the community as a whole. With the 21st-century learner in mind, some of the characteristics of the physical space should include the following as shown in Figure 8.4.

Program Administration by the Library Media Specialist

The library leader promotes sound program administration by ensuring sufficient staffing. An effective learner-centered elementary and secondary library media center should have at least one certified/licensed teacher-librarian and qualified clerical staff. Library staffing that accommodates the needs of the learning community must include a full-time clerk.

The library leader models flexible collaborative programming in the library. The teacher-librarian is always available to work with individuals, small groups, or whole classes in acquiring information literacy skills and reader's advisory in a flexible environment that allows team-teaching in the library, the classroom, or the computer lab. Librarians must work collaboratively with teachers (including the IT department) to align library resources to the curriculum. Good library leadership includes knowing what the teachers are teaching. Great leadership is modeling collaborative partnerships that integrate the state curriculum standards with units that meet the student's research needs. A checklist for success in collaboration might look something like Figure 8.5.

Figure 8.4 🙢 *Facility Space for 21st Century Learners*

Facility Space For 21st Century Learners

Technology Space	Multimedia Production Space	Informal Spaces
Desktop workstations adjacent to the computer lab/multimedia classroom supported by the IT (Instructional Technology) department working in collaboration with the library.	WiFi connections for individual and group work with a large projection screen and LCD projector. Room should be equipped with broadcast software loaded on all computers, allowing teachers and library staff to conduct instruction using individual laptops or large group instruction. (See definition at end of table.)	Project a comfortable relaxed atmosphere to informal spaces by adding armchairs, some in quiet, peaceful places where faculty can read and prepare; others in an open area where students can congregate, interact, and collaborate. Specialty lighting may be used to create atmosphere for the student area. The focus when selecting furniture and seating should build on partnership models that allow for collaborative activities.
WiFi (wireless) laptop workstations to be used for group and individual work.	Customized mouse-pads with library Web page URL for easy access to online resources.	Library space should communicate a welcoming ambience not only in terms of space, but also with a library staff that willingly gives assistance with technology and information use.
Easy access to the multimedia classroom for group presentations.	Enlist tech-savvy students to work as tech-assistants working to assist their peers as they use a variety of multimedia and software. Students work in tandem with the IT department and the library.	Students can be enlisted to serve on teams to advise and help design the informal space utilizing their creativity and imagination.
Tech-savvy students working as tech-assistants with their peers. Problems with mischievous students decrease as tech-assistants take pride in their work.	Develop a message board to help students know who else might be working on the same project, thus enabling a collaborative atmosphere to thrive.	Kiosks, placed in informal spaces, with interactive maps of the library and other vital portions of the school provide answers to common questions, and allow students to take an online tour of their learning environment. (See definition at end of table.)
Use of interactive tutorials to introduce different parts of the library to new students and teachers by highlighting electronic resources, online library catalog searching, or searching the Web. Students may work independently when using this kind of technology. (See definition at end of table.)	Computers should be loaded with the same software found throughout the school. This may include math simulation software to multimedia software.	Utilize student artwork and sculpture, as part of the permanent decoration for informal spaces. For example: Steel racks might be used to hang student-produced black and white photography in one area of an informal space.
Method to provide school faculty and administrators with professional development for use of online databases, digital, and multimedia software as well as computer-basics. Work with administration to make professional development part of the teacher technology proficiency for the year.	Both librarian and teacher work in a team-teaching situation to guide classes through interactive pathfinders utilizing streaming video, music clips, and URLs pertinent to the student's research needs.	

Figure 8.5 Ground Rules for Collaboration

Ground Rules for Collaboration	Classroom Teacher Responsibilities	Librarian Responsibilities
• Collaborative partnerships between classroom teacher and librarian are based upon shared goals. • Each partner executes a carefully defined role and is willing to change attitudes and expectations based upon shared goals. • Each partner contributes a unique element to the success of collaborative standards-based instruction. • Careful structural planning must occur between classroom teacher and librarian to create a team-teaching environment. • Collaborative program planning and team teaching are complex paradigm shifts requiring time to reach effective levels that impact student achievement.	• Prepare a syllabus to identify goals, teaching objectives, student outcomes, and assessment tools for the unit being developed. • Identify any existing resources already available in student textbook, Web sites, CD-ROMs, books. • Prepare to meet with the librarian during an uninterrupted block of time.	• Become familiar with the subject matter being taught by reading the textbook and completing preliminary periodical searches and Web searches. • Identify specific standards that align with the lesson being taught. • Find related standards and seek ways to integrate them across the curriculum. • Prepare to meet with the classroom teacher during an uninterrupted block of time. • Identify appropriate resources, electronic, print, and digital, that will support the lesson objectives.

The library leader collaborates with the Instructional Technology Team. As part of the leadership component in program administration, it is important to include the IT department as part of the collaborative planning process. With the emphasis on technology use in the classroom, the IT personnel will become an important component to the use of Web-based instruction, for they are the *guardians of the gateway… the network*. A good strong alliance with the IT department creates an indomitable partnership between the library and the IT department. Together, they (the librarian and the network administrator) create the new prototype for Educator X; that is, they are seen as professionals, each in their own right, who, in turn, are seen as "leaders and indispensable allies in educational restructuring" (Johnson, 2002).

The librarian is always available to work with the IT team to promote technology applications in all areas of the curriculum. A sound partnership should be developed to ensure integration of technology applications with library resources. The differences between the IT department and the library are very subtle. IT departments devote much of their time to building technical infrastructure and its support and maintenance, ensuring that the district's monetary investment is used to its maximum potential. Hence, less time can actually be spent on the learning outcomes of technology as they are related to the curriculum.

In cases where campuses have individuals designated as curriculum specialists—a specialized member of the technology team—the librarian has the opportunity to assist in the design of specific technology initiatives and proficiencies for their faculty. Librarians can take an active leadership role in helping the curriculum specialist prepare professional development for all departments.

In cases where there is no curriculum specialist, the professional development role falls to the teacher-librarian. The district has invested hundreds of thousands of dollars for technology infrastructure, yet they often neglect the investments of time and professional development needed to help teachers gain proficiency with the technologies the district has provided. By teaming together to provide professional development for teachers, librarians can demonstrate their ability to develop environments that are rich with content, which is standards-based. Teachers and administrators begin to see the librarian in a new light as a leader in the educational restructuring process (Johnson, 2002).

Furthermore, a collegial effort provides alignment to campus and district strategic plans, thus achieving the teaching and learning technology outcomes desired.

Program Administration Using Technology

The Library vs. the Web

The Web savvy library leader uses innovative methods to teach students how to locate quality digital information. Broadcast software allows teachers and library staff to simultaneously broadcast to all computers on the LAN. This kind of teaching methodology eliminates inattentive behavior. The master teaching station controls all LAN computers, and the entire class sees the demonstration on their individual computer screens. Once the demonstration has concluded, the students may resume their individualized research.

There are many virtual tours developed for students online. Librarians may use the same kind of visual orientation for their libraries. See the virtual tour of the Taj Mahal and other famous architectural buildings as examples at <http://www.taj-mahal.net/>.

Since NetGen students perceive the Web as their personal workspace and information universe, teacher-librarians should capitalize on this aspect. It is important to remember that students do not view the library and its resources as the loci of information; rather, they often times see it as an impenetrable barrier that requires too much energy to penetrate. The Colorado State University study on student search strategies noted that 59 percent of college freshman used a search engine to complete all of their research, while only 22 percent started with a library database (Kaminski et al., 2003, p. 5).

The Web savvy library leader creates Web portals and gateways that include digital images and multimedia links. In today's world, we find that the information search takes place virtually anywhere. In the past, much of the formal research had to be done in libraries with librarians assisting in the search process. Today, the information-seeker has become independent and relies only on a connection to the Web. In essence, information was a controlled entity in years past, but has become over-abundant today.

As a result of the profuse information environment, it becomes incumbent upon the library staff to assist the student in finding meaning in the sea of informational content. Recalling some of the characteristics of today's student, we know that they are visually kinesthetic, they have the ability to read digital imagery, and they expect a fast response time to their information needs. Those characteristics considered, the librarian may take a leadership role in creating a library Web page geared to the instructional needs of the NetGen student. Marc Prensky (2001) states today's students have developed *"hypertext minds"* as they have used technology in their formative years. They are looking for the most expeditious route to obtain all of their information, without regard to relevance or quality. Librarians can win the battle by easily creating Web portals or gateways that hinge off the Web-based library catalog. Providing the "one-stop shopping" or federated searching for Web-based research allows the student to search the Web, the library databases, the library catalog, and even multimedia libraries simultaneously; Thus, the student has the same global searching experience that a single search engine might offer. However, the quality of digital information is much more useful because the search takes place in a controlled, relevant environment. With guided instruction, students can learn the good mechanics of a search strategy, and become discriminating users of the information they find. There are those detractors who argue that *one-stop* searching, or federated searching, limits the information that students would find if they were to use multiple searches. For veteran researchers, using only one source (in this case, the Web) is limiting and binding. However, for young minds that are developing cognitive reasoning skills, guiding the search can prove to be useful if the students understand the kinds of databases and links that will yield success in learning.

Database companies are seeing the need to federate searching by using the library Web page as a portal for information retrieval. Considering the visual aptitude and the *hypertext minds* of today's users, we see a change in Web page development. New visual display interfaces drive the meta-search engines as they search the Web. These specialized meta-search engines launch the query to a set of search engines, gather the results, compile them, and represent them in a series of interactive maps that the user can browse. This kind of a visual display tool promotes the use of visual acuity so many students have developed as the millennial generation. Think of these kinds of search engines as *invisible librarians* that gather information and bring it back electronically for the searcher to use.

If a student were researching the Holocaust, the visual display of the search results might look something like Figure 8.6.

Figure 8.6 *Visual Display*

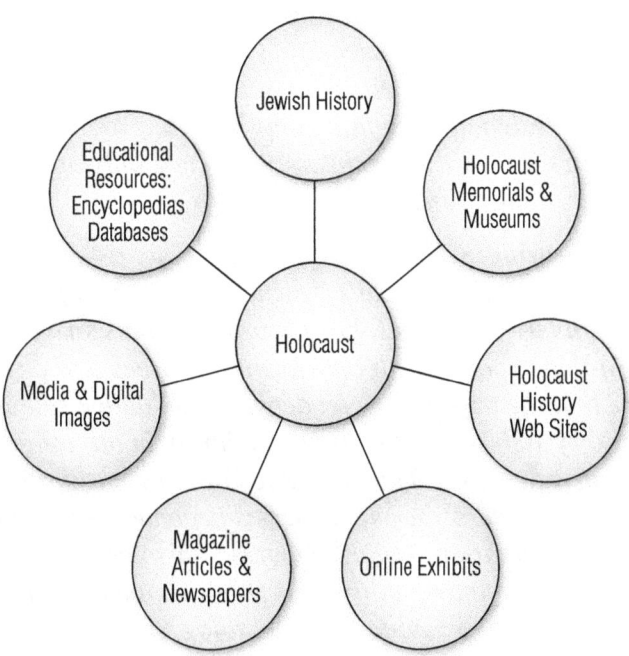

Such search tools can optimize student learning by providing a supportive environment while facilitating student independence as they learn correct search strategies. Think of the federated search as training wheels for online searching. Remember, however, that the first people a librarian must train regarding correct search strategies are their own colleagues. Building an awareness and knowledge of the electronic resources, and how to access them through a library Web portal is vital. Introducing teachers to the idea that information literacy starts with them is tantamount to good leadership.

The Internet librarian creates Web pages that are concise and easy to use. Some of the basic ideas to consider when creating a Web page for instructional purposes include the following:

- ***Design:*** *Remember that the design itself should never obstruct the flow of information. The World Wide Web Consortium (W3C), founded by Tim Berners-Lee, has created guidelines for Web page development. The W3C has prepared an excellent checklist to use when reviewing a page or Web site for its accessibility. A few of the major points are listed below.*

- ***Usability:*** *All populations of the school: special education students, special needs patrons such as those with visual or physical impairments, senior citizens, and ESL students should be able to use the Web page with ease. A good library Web page should reflect the needs of the school community and its users (including the parent community).*

- ***Font size:*** *Does the online catalog and the Web page have fonts that are easily readable? Don't use fonts that have only subtle differences. Make the user buttons large for ease of use as well. Make sure that labels on buttons or graphics do not wrap. Students using magnification devices to assist in visual perception may not see the entire label.*

- ***Graphics:*** *Consider the connection speed of users both on campus and off. Some students (or rather their parents), especially off-campus, still have dial-up connections, so graphics do not load as easily as those with a broadband connection. Graphics can be a problem for the visually impaired as well, since some students cannot distinguish between the design and the functionality of the Web page features. You may want to give your users the option of text only appearances if they have slower connections.*

- ***Invisible librarian:*** *Create the Web page to act as an invisible librarian, making the student's "swim through the information sea" easier for the user. After all, library professionals strive to maintain an "open-door" policy with their print resources and physical space. It is time that the true library leader takes an active role in the design of his library Web site to ensure accessibility in all arenas. Web site design expert Susanna Davidsen (2004) writes "A library's website is no longer an add-on service, but has become the library's presence to more and more users" (n.p.). Davidsen also points out that the library Web site's functionality is as significant as library signage, the circulation desk, or even the online catalog.*

- *Library jargon:* Advocacy for libraries has developed an understood maxim: If you want the world to know what you do and to understand the library world then avoid library jargon! W3C recommends that Web page sentences use simple sentence structure. Try to use the simplest and cleanest sentence structure appropriate for the site's contents.

- *Relevant keyword:* Write links that use relevant keywords. Try to use keywords that are commonly used.

- *Web accessibility verifiers:* W3C has established guidelines for software called Web Accessibility that checks Web pages for their accessibility. Information about accessibility tools can be found at the federal government site: <http://www.usdoj.gov/crt/508/web.htm> .

(Note: WAVE, <www.wave.webaim.org/index.jsp>) is a free-ware that offers an assessment of the library Web site as well as a transaction tool that logs the frequency of Web sites accessed. Another Web validation tool is A-Prompt Toolkit, <http://aprompt.snow.utoronto.ca/> developed by the University of Toronto and the Trace Center at the University of Wisconsin.)

The tech-savvy library leader creates opportunities to connect teachers and electronic resources in the library. OCLC (2004) states that the number of worldwide digital resources available to education in 2004 is 5,400,000. By the conclusion of 2009 that number is projected to jump to 42,100,000. With those kinds of numbers, libraries need to become proactive in educating teachers to the kind and use of electronic resources in their libraries. Research indicates that teachers are the vital link to their students using quality resources in the research process.

The Pew Internet report has established that 80 percent of students aged 12 to 18 prefer to use the free Internet, even when their schools provide online encyclopedias and subject specific databases for their use. Although research is still in its infancy, there is great suspicion among professionals in the library field that teachers are the vital link between students Googling their research and students who utilize authoritative digital resources such as subscription databases and other electronic resources; indeed, we may say that teachers dictate, to a great degree, the resources students will be permitted to use.

Hence, a teacher who is informed and practiced in the use of a specific electronic database, will in turn, require that their students be informed as well. It then becomes the job of the teacher-librarian to develop a program that will increase the awareness of electronic resources available to their school community. How is this done? Surveys, benchmarks, and professional development sessions!

Case Study F

Start with a survey to set the benchmark for future data the library may collect on the use of electronic resources. Survey questions should allow the library staff to get a realistic picture of the faculty's technology proficiencies. Use an online survey or scantron sheet to rank teachers' answers. (Once the library has gathered all of the data, one of the math classes could be enlisted to create a table listing the percentage of answers for each question. The information could then be presented to the school administrator as they plan their professional development sessions.)

Here are some sample questions that could be included in the benchmark survey. (For additional ideas and questions that can be included in the benchmark survey go to the government Web site <http://www.usdoj.gov/crt/508/web.htm>.)

Electronic Resources

- *With which electronic resources are you familiar?*
- *Subscription databases (List the databases individually to get an accurate picture of the teacher's awareness of that specific resource.)*
- *Digital encyclopedias*
- *Internet*
- *Library catalog*
- *Library Web page*

Student Use of Electronic Resources

- *Which electronic resource do you feel is more reliable for student research?*
- *Which electronic resource do you direct students to use most often?*
- *How often do you direct your students to use the Internet?*
- *What percentage of student research utilizes the electronic resource?*
- *Who is responsible for teaching your students about the electronic resource?*
- *What percentage of your students understands constructing a search strategy using Boolean logic?*
- *How often do your students visit the library during the school year?*
- *How often do you consult with the library to plan a specific lesson?*

Teacher Technology Proficiency vs. Student Proficiency

- *How often do you let your students choose their own resources for a research project?*
- *How often do you direct them to ask the teacher-librarian for instructional help?*
- *How often do you direct students to use print resources as their only source?*
- *How often do you direct students to use the Internet as their only source?*
- *How often do you direct your students to use subscription databases? Before using the Internet? After using the Internet?)*
- *How often do you direct your students not to use the Internet at all during the research process?*
- *How often do you use the Internet in your instruction?*
- *How often do you use the Internet outside your work?*
- *How often do you use e-mail?*

Organizational Professional Development Strategies

- *Based upon your use of technology, which kind of learning strategy would best suit your needs?*
- *Once a year?*
- *Twice per year?*
- *Departmental sessions held monthly throughout the school year?*
- *Department sessions held at the beginning of the year before school commences?*
- *Large group sessions taught by the library staff using PowerPoint and handouts?*
- *Synchronous training taught on a monthly basis?*
- *Synchronous training taught once per year?*
- *Individualized instruction?*
- *E-mail communication regarding resources and how to use them?*

Based on the answers to this survey, the library staff and the administration should plan together to deliver professional development that will enhance the technology skills of the campus faculty. Provision of electronic resource training does several things: (1) creates an awareness in the teacher's mind of resources that will enhance their curriculum; (2) allows the teacher to model the same research methodology they expect from their students; and (3) creates a collaborative relationship between themselves and the library staff that allows for the creation of standards-based research projects.

The library leader uses guided instruction linked to state curriculum standards to enhance student learning. Librarians must work collaboratively with teachers (including the IT department) to align library resources to the curriculum. Again, good library leadership is knowing what the teachers are teaching. Great leadership is knowing the state curriculum standards and then, in a collaborative arena, working with the teacher to develop units that meet the student's research needs. In the past, librarians have developed pathfinders to assist and direct the student to a particular grouping of resources. Just a few years ago, these pathfinders consisted of print resources exclusively. Today, pathfinders combine print and electronic resources such as Web links, video-clip links, online games and quizzes, and much more. However, one universal problem still remains: Teachers rarely know that the pathfinder exists, and today's student see it as an unwanted accessory to their assignments. They neither want the time-consuming job of executing and digesting the information contained in the pathfinder nor do they feel it necessary for an A-grade. Why? Because it's not part of the teacher's assignment. Thus, we find the library disconnected once again unless efforts are made to include the pathfinder as part of the teacher's assignment to the students.

Using the assignment link as a useful strategy brings the world of information to students in an arena that is relevant to their needs…their research assignment! The Library of Congress has some excellent examples of pathfinders on its Learning Page. (See the Library of Congress Portals Application Group Web page for latest developments in the field of information literacy and trends at <http://memory.loc.gov/learn/start/gs_src_path.html>. In addition to Library of Congress, the Internet Public Library at <http://www.ipl.org/> offers some excellent pathfinder links. Currently, the development of Google Scholar, a project from Stanford University, aims to bring resources together in a dynamic search that allows the user to browse many resources simultaneously.

Program Administration Beyond the Library Walls

A library leader actively participates in leadership roles on the campus and district level. Participation in school or district leadership committees and councils are excellent methods to promote and share the positive student outcomes of an effective library program.

A library leader knows the curriculum needs and asks for suggestions from teachers and administrators. Good collection development supports the curriculum. When purchasing materials utilized by teachers and students, ask for input from staff and faculty members. Add URLs that are accurate and part of the collection development process. Use good collection development guidelines for Web site collection as well.

A library leader objectively assesses and collects data regarding the library program to create the impetus for change. The teacher-librarian willingly solicits and learns from criticisms and suggestions by surveying all participants—staff, students, and parents—to learn where improvements can be made in the library. Great library leadership requires effort and commitment to accurate data collection. Collection of data that demonstrate program effectiveness can be shared with appropriate members of the administration and results used to forecast and plan for the future. Statistical measurements can provide a framework for self-assessment and strategic planning. For example, the Standards and Guidelines for Texas 2005, <http://www.tsl.state.tx.us/ld/schoollibs/index.html>, recently rewritten, provides assessment for three aspects of the library program. They are:

> *1) Strategies for Librarians—a category that assesses the level of library's resources and services.*
>
> *2) Output Measures—assess the level of use of the library program.*
>
> *3) Evidence-Based Measures—assess the impact of school library resources/services on student achievement and determine the operating level of the library program.*

For example, Texas school librarians have begun to gather statistical profiles of their libraries to demonstrate the direct impact libraries have on student achievement. Standards and Guidelines for Texas provides a framework for self-assessment and strategic planning for the library program. The Strategies for Librarians assess the level of resources and services of the library program and refer to supplemental resources for quantitative and qualitative measurement of the library program. The supplemental resources are 1) Output Measures that assess the level of use of the library program, and 2) Evidence-Based Measures that assess level of success of the school library program in supporting students in learning the state mandated curriculum, the Texas Essential Knowledge and Skills (TEKS), and demonstrating mastery of that curriculum on the state mandated test, the Texas Assessment of Knowledge and Skills (TAKS). Evaluation of a library program based on the Strategies for Librarians, Output Measures, and Evidence-Based Measures may be used for planning, improving the library program, and measuring success in achieving the program goal of supporting student achievement.

Output Measures for school library programs are provided as supplemental resources that may be used to quantify the level of use of library programs and services by staff, students, and the community. Outputs are quantities of resources and activities that the library program provides in order to fulfill its mission. They measure program productivity. When compared year-to-year, Output Measures show how usage of the services and resources of the library program has changed over time. Seven Output Measures are recommended as supplemental resources to the Standards and Guidelines for Texas. Instructions for Data Collection, a Data Collection Sheet, and a Worksheet for Calculating Output Measures are included in the Output Measures section of the Texas School Library Standards.

> Measure 1. Percentage of Planning Requests Filled or Modified
>
> Measure 2. Percentage of Teaching Requests Filled or Modified
>
> Measure 3. Percentage of Curriculum Requests Addressed with Print Resources
>
> Measure 4. Percentage of Curriculum Requests Addressed with Internet Resources
>
> Measure 5. Percentage of Curriculum Requests Addressed with Subscription Databases
>
> Measure 6. Average Number of Print Resources Utilized Per Student Per Week
>
> Measure 7. Average Number of Print, Internet, and Subscription Databases Utilized Per Student Per Week

The seven Output Measures were developed based on information provided in the book, *Output Measures for School Library Media Programs* by Frances Bryant Bradburn (1999).

Evidenced-Based Measures for school library programs are provided as supplemental resources that may be used to determine the impact of the library program on student achievement. Evidence-Based Evaluation is a systematic method of assessing the extent to which a program has achieved its intended result. Student achievement is the objective of school library programs. The Evidence-Based Evaluation Plan included as a supplemental resource to the Standards and Guidelines for Texas is designed to assess the impact of school library resources and services on student achievement. Evidence-Based Evaluation answers two important questions:

1) How has the library program made a difference to students, and 2) How are students better off as a result of experiencing the library program?

The Evidence-Based Measures included as supplemental resources are designed to reveal 1) the extent to which the library program supports student learning of the state mandated curriculum, Texas Essential Knowledge and Skills (TEKS), and 2) the extent of student success in meeting the passing standard on the state-mandated exams, Texas Assessment of Knowledge and Skills (TAKS), as a result of library instruction.

Three Evidenced-Based Measures are used to assess the success of the library program in achieving these goals.

Evidence-based Measure 1: Students and staff have increased access during and beyond the instructional day to a balanced, carefully selected, and systematically organized collection of current and relevant print and electronic library resources that are sufficient to meet their needs in support of mastering Texas Essential Knowledge and Skills (TEKS) student expectations in all subject areas.

Evidence-based Measure 2: Students and staff gain increased knowledge of TEKS student expectations through ongoing instruction in the integration of information technology and information literacy as planned and presented collaboratively by teachers and librarians.

Evidence-based Measure 3: Students' Texas Assessment of Knowledge and Skills (TAKS) scores demonstrate achievement as related to the TEKS student expectations that are selected for improvement and either taught by the librarian individually or in collaboration with other teachers. See Figure 8.7: Evidence-based Measures below.

Figure 8.7 — *Evidence-based Measures*

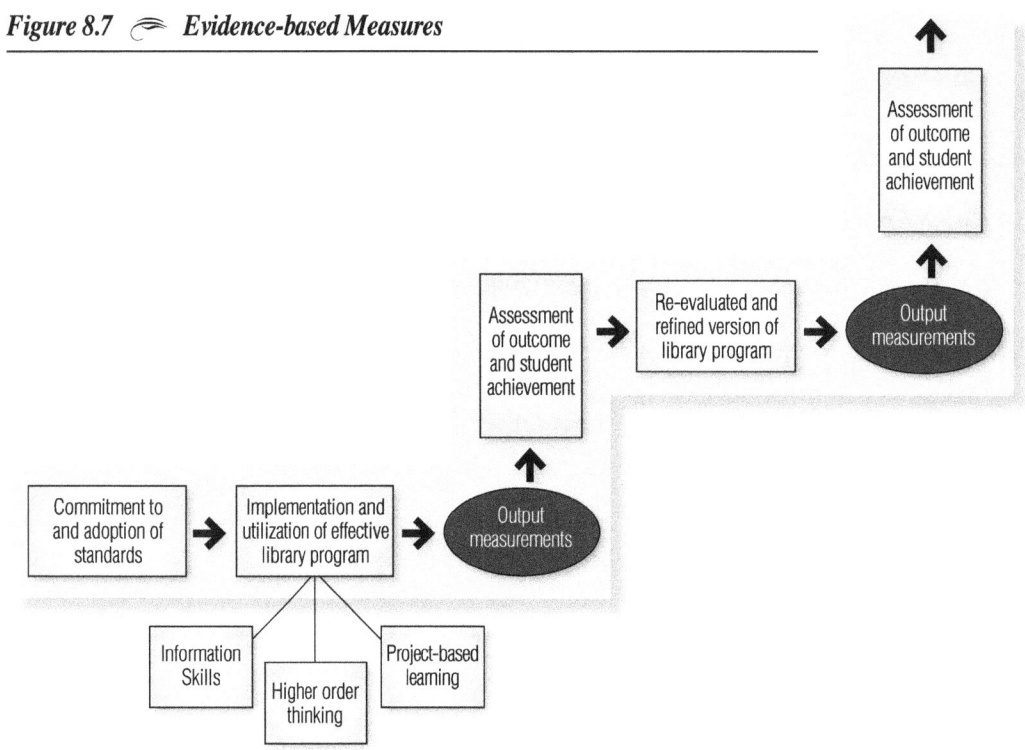

When school libraries begin to target student achievement in terms of learner-centered programming, the school library impacts learning in a new and powerful way. The bottom line is simply this: Librarians who infuse their libraries with programs and services that are standard-based and learner-centered, create a dynamic environment that cultivates students' active participation in their own learning.

Finally, remember that assuming the role of a leader and shaping a current library program is an ongoing process. Apply patience and applaud accomplishments, embryonic as they may be. As library program reshaping begins, remember the sage advice of Sir Winston Churchill, "Every day you may make progress. Every step may be fruitful. Yet there will stretch out before you an ever-lengthening, ever-ascending, every-improving path. You know you will never get to the end of the journey. But this, so far from discouraging, only adds to the joy and glory of the climb." ~Sir Winston Churchill 1874-1965

Works Cited

American Association of School Librarians, & Association for Educational Communications and Technology. (1998). *Information power: Building partnerships for learning.* Chicago: American Library Association.

Bradburn, F. B. *Output measures for school library media programs.* Neal-Schuman, 1999.

Davidsen, S. & Yankee, E. *Web site design with the patron in mind: A step-by-step guide for libraries.* Chicago: American Library Association, 2004.

Digital-age literacy. enGAUGE. North Central Regional Educational Laboratory. Retrieved Sept. 24, 2004 from http://www.ncrel.org/engauge/skills/agelit.htm

Ediger, Marlow. The school library and the learner. *Research in Education.* Jul 2004.

Johnson, D. (1997) The indespensable librarians surviving (and thriving) in school media centers in the information age. Worthington, OH: Linworth.

Johnson, D. (2002) The indespenable teacher's guide to computer skills. Worthington, OH: Linworth.

Kaiser Family Foundation. New study finds children age zero to six spend as much time with TV, computers, and video games as playing outside. Online posting. 28 Oct 2003. Henry J. Kaiser Family Foundation. 17 Jun 2005. http://www.kff.org/entrmedia/entmedia102803nr.cfm.

Kaminski, K., Seel, P., & Cullen, K. *Educause Quarterly*, No. 3, 2003.

Oblinger, D. and J. IS it age or IT: First steps toward understanding the net generation. Educating the net generation. Feb. 2005. EDUCAUSE. Retrieved Jun 27, 2005 from <http://www.educause.edu>

OCLC 2004 Information format trends: Content not context. OCLC Online Computer Library Center. Report, May 2004.

O'Reilly, B. Meet the Millennial Generation. *Fortune* 24 Jul 2000: 142.: 144-48, 150, 154, 156, 160, 162, 168.

Pew Internet. The digital disconnect: The widening gap between Internet-savvy students and their schools. Online posting. 14 Aug 2002. Pew Internet & American Life Project 17 Jun 2005. <http://www.pewinternet.org/PPF/r/67/report_display.asp>

Prensky, M. Digital natives, digital immigrants part II: Do they really think differently? *On the Horizon*: NCB University Press. Vol. 9 No. 6 Dec 2001.

Scribner. Jay Padres. Do-it-yourselfers or engineers: Bricolage as a metaphor for teacher work and learning. *Research in Education,* Feb 2004:15.

Wagner, T. Change as collaborative inquiry: A constructivist methodology for reinventing schools. Phi Delta *Kappan* March 1998: 512-15

Washington Post 31 July 2002:C01.

World Wide Web Consortium http://www.w3.org/

CHAPTER NINE: EVALUATION and REFLECTION

Mary Lankford

In a fable about mice having problems with a cat, the mice decide that if the cat wore a bell the mice would be forewarned and could avoid problems with the cat. The problem then became: Who will bell the cat? Consider this problem when thinking of being evaluated by the principal. We are not advocating placing a bell on the principal, but the more you know and understand about the role of the principal in the school the more readily the librarian can prepare to inform, educate, and be evaluated by the principal.

Books, articles, and current studies continue to reinforce the necessity for leadership in education. In *Better Leadership for America's Schools: A Manifesto* (2003) published by The Broad Foundation, Thomas B. Fordham Institute, problems are identified; successful leaders are named; and an overview of administrator certification is provided. School librarians should locate this document and make it available to building administrators. It can be found at http://www.edexcellence.net/institute/publication/publication.cfm?id=1.

> If two decades of research into school effectiveness have reached any reliable conclusion, it's that successful schools invariably have dynamic, savvy, and focused leaders—women and men who are capable of rallying educators, parents, children, and community members to achieve shared goals. Yet far too many U.S. schools and school districts lack such helmsmen. *(Better Leadership for America's Schools: A Manifesto, 2003, p. 2).*

Better Leadership for America's Schools: A Manifesto does not mention a librarian by name, but I read librarian, between the lines, in this citation.

> There's no denying that a school's principal is responsible for its instructional leadership, along with much else. The core of the job is ensuring a high quality curriculum, effective teaching in every classroom, and satisfactory academic performance by the school's pupils. But that does not mean the principal must be the "best" teacher or "principal teacher" in the school. He or she may assume this task directly or may instead function as the school's CEO, delegating to others—a vice principal, head teacher or dean of instruction—the weighty and complex task of designing, delivering, and supervising curriculum and instruction (p. 22-23).

As I read through this excellent document I added librarian to the people cited. The librarian is involved with all the tasks included in the quote. Once again, it is up to the librarian to advocate being a leader in the school's performance.

The Council of Chief State School Officers [CCSSO] is a nationwide nonprofit organization composed of the public officials who head departments of elementary and secondary education in the states, the District of Columbia, the Department of Defense Education Activity, and five extra-state jurisdictions. CCSSO, in November 1996, published "Standards for School Leaders." Each of the six standards identifies knowledge on which the standard is based and dispositions or the values and beliefs the administrators hold, followed by performance indicators for the standard. The CCSSO Standards are included so that librarians will have a better understanding of the performance standards identified by Chief State School Officers. Not only does the librarian need to be aware of this document, the librarian should make school administrators aware of the document.

> **Standard 1:** A school administrator is an educational leader who promotes the success of all students by facilitating the development, articulation, implementation, and stewardship of a vision of learning that is shared and supported by the school community.
>
> **Standard 2:** A school administrator is an educational leader who promotes the success of all students by advocating, nurturing, and sustaining a school culture and instructional program conducive to student learning and staff professional growth.
>
> **Standard 3:** A school administrator is an educational leader who promotes the success of all students by ensuring management of the organization, operations, and resources for a safe, efficient, and effective learning environment.
>
> **Standard 4:** A school administrator is an educational leader who promotes the success of all students by collaborating with families and community members, responding to diverse community interests and needs, and mobilizing community resources.
>
> **Standard 5:** A school administrator is an educational leader who promotes the success of all students by acting with integrity, fairness, and in an ethical manner.
>
> **Standard 6:** A school administrator is an educational leader who promotes the success of all students by understanding, responding to, and influencing the larger political, social, economic, legal, and cultural context (CCSSO, 1996, p. 10).

Each librarian should have a file established for articles on leadership. Reading is the act of reinforcement of ideas and tasks, and will serve as a reminder of leadership skills and how to build those skills. In Paul Johnson's (2005) article "Five Marks of a Great Leader" he states, "In both business and politics leadership matters more than does any other personal factor. A Country with a first-class leader can punch above its weight class (look at Britain under Margaret Thatcher). Admiration for a company's chairman/CEO is sure to be reflected in the share price.

The Interstate School Leader's Licensure Consortium (ISLLC) Standards were developed by the Council of Chief State School Offices (CCSSO) and member states. Copies may be downloaded from the Council's website at ww.ccsso.org (they only have two w's). Council of Chief State School Offices (1996). *Interstate School Leader's Licensure Consortium (ISLLC) Standards for School Leaders*. Washington, D.C.: Author.

But what makes a real leader? How can we recognize one?" (p. 3)
A real leader might have:

- *moral courage,*
- *judgment,*
- *a sense of priority,*
- *the disposal and concentration of effort, and*
- *humor.*

Use technology within your library to locate and read the entire article. The author's expansion of terms is an excellent guide. The author did not rank the attributes listed, and they are all important. Too often humor is not included as a characteristic of leadership. Think first of a smile, then add a touch of humor to almost any situation. Humor (if not used in a sarcastic manner) will create a relaxed atmosphere, and lead to more *civilized* meetings.

How do you evaluate how much the school administration understands about the library program? It has been said that, "Principals' daily work is characterized by brevity, variety, fragmentation, complexity, ambiguity, and uncertainty." If we use this description of a principal's day, how does the librarian approach the question of informing and educating the principal? It is estimated that the daily work of a principal may include 2,000 separate interactions a day. Their work, just as the work of the librarian, is fraught with interruption. This description should eliminate a request for a "moment" of the administrator's time. If the librarian establishes goals for the school year those goals should be based on the principal's basic concern: to improve student achievement.

As a library leader do not look at small pieces of the library program, but at the overall design of a program that assists the principal in that basic goal: improving student achievement.

List problems the library program faces. Be certain these are real problems, not irritations that the librarian, with the help of teachers and students, can resolve. Problems include:

- *dated, worn, inadequate collection of books,*
- *insufficient space for the library program activities,*
- *a rigid schedule that does not allow access to library resources, and*
- *inadequate technology for student and teacher use.*

Remember that all of these problems require long-range solutions; data that support the problem; and a thoughtful evaluation of how the problem can be resolved.

What problem has the highest priority? What problem must be resolved with additional funding? How have other schools in the district resolved the problems? Are there grant funds that would allow the problem to be solved? Is there someone in the district (other than the principal) who can assist in grant applications, or information on funding through district bond funds, or federal funds?

Librarian Certification

Is there a copy of the certification standards for school librarians in your state on file in the principal's office? The Maine Association of School Libraries Web site <http://www.maslibraries.org/> includes an Evaluation-Action Plan and an Evaluation Kit. This Kit includes an excellent form for the librarian to use prior to an evaluation. The suggestion is made that this be included with documentation prior to the evaluation. The paragraph preceding the form says, "As a leader, planner and manager, the Library Media Specialist provides leadership in the planning, management and evaluation of school library media programs." Examples focus on the element most relevant to the indicator.

Certification and State School Library Standards

The foundation for evaluation of school librarians should be based on state certification guidelines. Both the principal and librarian should maintain current copies of these documents. Many librarians may be "grandfathered" in to the latest certification standards; however, both administrators and librarians should be aware of the latest standards and how they affect the library program. Some states have integrated certification requirements for the librarian in school library standards. Texas is a good example of the full circle of school librarian certification, state school library standards, and evaluation instruments developed by school districts based on these documents. The certification and School Library Standards for Texas school librarians can also be seen on the Texas State Library Web site at <http://www.tsl.state.tx.us/ld/schoollibs/#main>.

Portfolio Development

Creative librarians can easily develop a portfolio of what happens in the library. A digital and video camera meshed into a PowerPoint program will easily demonstrate projects and student utilization of the library. Why a portfolio? Marilyn S. Heath answers questions about portfolios in her book *Electronic Portfolios: A Guide to Professional Development and Assessment*. Heath (2004) describes a professional portfolio as: "An organized collection of self-selected artifacts and self-generated reflections, developed for a specific purpose and audience that demonstrate the author's professional knowledge, skills, dispositions, and growth over time" (p. 7). The portfolio may be used as part of an evaluation performance, or as a visual part of a resume and job application. The development of a portfolio requires the librarian to focus on the important aspects of the library program and shows professional growth. Self-evaluation and reflection are important parts of providing feedback as you assess your work.

Librarians assume the role of instructor in so many ways. In *Information Anxiety 2* the author, Richard Saul Wurman (2000), states:

> Corporations are responding by empowering people to make their own decisions. They are empowering people to find their way, to navigate through information, products, and comments about products. You can go to barnesandnoble.com and Amazon.com and write your own reviews. This gives you freedom to find out things. This is why we created libraries. The Library of Alexandria was man's knowledge in one place—the core of civilization. And now we have it in everybody's home, at everybody's desk. We are empowered in an astonishing way, and certainly our economy is based now on that freedom of searching and finding sources, the freedom of finding out (p. 292).

Reflection

One of the definitions for reflection is "serious thought or consideration" *(New Oxford, 2005)*. Utilizing the amazing number of technological tools we have at our disposal I think the time for reflection is essential for us to "ground" ourselves in our world. A title recently recommended to me by a librarian was *The World Is Flat, A Brief History of the Twenty-First Century,* by Thomas L. Friedman. For those working with technology this book should be on your reading list. Friedman (2005) tells us:

> ...where we are going to see the digitization, virtualization, and automation of almost everything. The gains in productivity will be staggering for those countries, companies, and individuals who can absorb the new technological tools. And we are entering a phase where more people than ever before in the history of the world are going to have access to these tools—as innovators, as collaborators, and, alas, even as terrorists. You say you want a revolution? Well, the real information revolution is about to begin (p. 45). Leadership in libraries will become more and more important.

If you want a very clear presentation of this topic, *The Smallest Ever Guide to the Internet for Busy People* by Nigel Holmes is an excellent example of "information architecture" and certainly makes a complex topic very understandable. Another topic Wurman discusses is "Latch: The Five Ultimate Hayracks." As librarians we understand that the many ways of organizing information are finite. Wurman (2000) says:

> It can only be organized by location, alphabet, time, category, or hierarchy. These modes are applicable to almost any endeavor—from your personal file cabinets to multinational corporations. They are the framework upon which annual reports, books, conversations, exhibitions, directories, conventions, and even warehouses are arranged. While information may be infinite, the ways of structuring it are not. And once you have a place in which the information can be plugged, it becomes that much more useful. Your choice will be determined by the story you want to tell. Each way will permit a different understanding of the information—within each are many variations. However, recognizing that the main choices are limited makes the process less intimidating (p. 40).

The library leader communicates the importance of location to students and teachers. In the book one librarian uses the acronym L.A.T.C.H. to represent Location, Alphabet, Category, and Hierarchy. The librarian must create understanding of methods of organization in order to save time for researchers. "Understanding the structure and organization of information permits you to extract value and significance from it" (Wurman, 2000, p. 42). The critical attributes of information organization must be very high on the list of skills students must acquire.

Among the many interesting facts Friedman points out is the brief history of technology. Major technology events have happened in our lifetime. The first IBM PC hit the market in 1981 (Friedman, 2005, p. 53). Windows 3.0 was shipped on May 22, 1990. Does it seem possible that all this has happened to our world since the mid 1980s? Friedman also points out that although "we may take browser technology for granted, it was actually one of the most important inventions in modern history" (Friedman, 2005, p. 40).

You may believe you are running as fast as you can, but you can not slow down. Friedman (2005) compares 11/9 and 9/11 in his book. The date the Berlin Wall came down was 11/9. Friedman states:

> We Americans will have to work harder, run faster, and become smarter to make sure we get our share. But let us not underestimate our strengths or the innovation that could explode from the flat world when we really do connect all of the knowledge centers together. On such a flat earth, the most important attribute you can have is creative imagination—the ability to be the first on your block to figure out how all these enabling tools can be put together in new and exciting way to create products, communities, opportunities, and profits. That has always been America's strength, because America was, and for now still is, the world's greatest dream machine" (Friedman, 2005, p. 42).

There is no better place to allow young people to dream and imagine than the library. There are no better people than librarians to lead young people into the world of the future through the technology and books available in the library.

Works Cited

Better Leadership for America's Schools: A Manifesto. (2003). The Broad Foundation, Thomas B. Fordham Insitute. Maine Association of School Libraries Evaluation-Action Plan and Evaluation Kit. http://www.maslibraries.org/

Council of Chief State School Officers. (1996). *Interstate School Leaders Licensure Consortium (ISLLC) Standards for School Leaders.* Washington, DC: Author. Available: http://www.ccsso.org/content/pdfs/isllcstd.pdf

Friedman, T. L. (2005). *World is flat: A brief history of the twenty-first century.* New York: Farrar, Straus & Giroux.

Heath, M. S. (2004). *Electronic portfolios: A guide to professional development and assessment.* Worthington, OH: Linworth Publishing.

Johnson, P. (2005). Five marks of a great leader. *Forbes,* May 9, 2005 n.p.

The New Oxford American Dictionary (2nd ed.). (2005). New York: Oxford University Press.

Wurman, R. S. (2000). *Information anxiety 2.* Indianapolis, IN: Que.

www.ingramcontent.com/pod-product-compliance
Lightning Source LLC
Chambersburg PA
CBHW081830300426
44116CB00014B/2539